HISTORY OF INVENTION

COMMUNICATION AND COMPUTERS

COMMUNICATION AND COMPUTERS

Chris Woodford

Facts On File, Inc.

Facts On File, Inc.
132 West 31st Street
New York, NY 10001

Library of Congress Cataloging-in-Publication Data

Woodford, Chris
   Communication and Computers / Chris Woodford.
    p. cm.
   Summary: Discusses how communication has changed from the first written language and the use of paper through advances using the spoken word and moving images to the development and widespread uses of computers.
   Includes bibliographical references and index.
   ISBN 0-8160-5443-6
   1. Telecommunication—Juvenile literature.
2. Computers—Juvenile literature. [1. Communication.
2. Telecommunication. 3. Computers.] I. Title.

TK5102.4.W66 2004
004—dc22

2003021114

Facts On File books are available at special discounts when purchased in bulk quantities for businesses, associations, institutions, or sales promotions. Please call our Special Sales Department in New York at (212) 967-8800 or (800) 322-8755.

You can find Facts On File on the World Wide Web at http://www.factsonfile.com

For The Brown Reference Group plc:
Project Editor: Tom Jackson
Design: Bradbury and Williams
Picture Research: Becky Cox
Managing Editor: Bridget Giles
Consultant: Dr. Thomas Haigh, History and Sociology
   of Science, University of Pennsylvania, Philadelphia.

Printed and bound in Singapore

10 9 8 7 6 5 4 3 2 1

CONTENTS

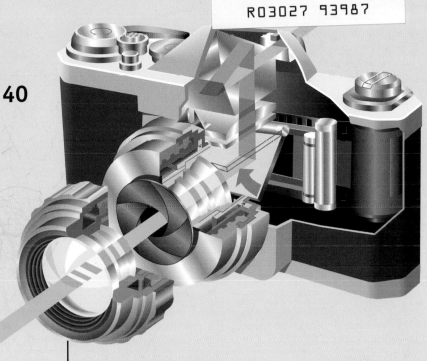

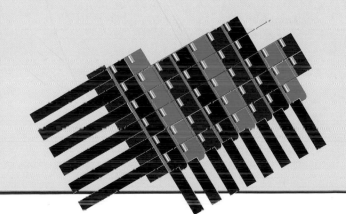

For centuries no one knew how to read Egyptian writing. In 1799, the Rosetta Stone was found. This had both Greek and Egyptian writing on it and was used to translate Egyptian for the first time.

All animals communicate, but only people have developed the ability to speak and write using language. While speech makes it possible for people to express their ideas more easily, writing is arguably the most important of all human inventions: It allows us to record our ideas and knowledge so other people can learn from them.

THE BIRTH OF WRITING

The earliest writing was quite different from the writing in use today, but its purpose was exactly the same: to communicate ideas and record information. People have been communicating ideas since prehistoric times, when they first made rock drawings or carved marks into rocks. People started to

Key inventions

Papyrus to Paper

Written languages would have been useless without things to write on. It was the ancient Egyptians who invented paper, about 3000 B.C.E. They discovered they could draw ink onto a paperlike material (above, a religious text) made from the stem of the papyrus plant. The Greeks and Romans also used papyrus, but it was replaced by parchment and vellum in the fourth century. Parchment was a strong material made from treated animal skin. Vellum was a finer writing material made from freshly killed animals.

Paper, as we know it today, was first made from tree bark in 105 C.E. in China by Ts'ai Lun (50–118 C.E.). The technology of papermaking arrived in Europe in the 12th century when the first papermaking factory (or mill) was built in Spain. America's first paper mill was constructed in 1690. Today, paper is made with enormous rotary mills called Fourdrinier machines, named for the English brothers Henry (1766–1854) and Sealy Fourdrinier (1774–1847), who developed the modern papermaking process in 1803.

record information systematically when they decided to keep written accounts of trade and taxes. This was first done about 10,000 years ago in Babylon (in modern-day Iraq) and ancient Egypt. These early records were marks made on bones and clay tablets.

PICTURES AND WORDS

Written language was invented when people found ways of writing down the kinds of things they had always been able to say out loud. There are two very different ways of writing. One represents things as pictures, the other as words.

The simplest form of written language is called pictography, or picture writing. Native American people were among the first to use it. Native Americans often moved from place to place, and it was not always easy to speak with people belonging to other tribes who did not speak the same language. Native people who lived on the Great Plains developed two ways of solving this problem. Instead of speaking, they used simple hand gestures that other tribes could easily understand. Instead of writing with letters and words, they drew simplified

The Phaistos Disk

Early in the 20th century, archaeologists discovered a mysterious clay disk in the ruins of a palace at Phaistos on the Greek island of Crete. The disk (right) seems to date from 1700 B.C.E. On each side of the disk, which is about 6 inches (16 cm) across, there is a message written in a spiral pattern. It consists of 100 small pictures that are broken up by lines into what seem to be words or phrases. Forty-five different symbols are used in the message, including pictures of men, women, fish, birds, and tools. Each of these pictures is identically printed everywhere it occurs. So the symbols must have been pressed into the clay using wooden or metal punches. This would make the disk the oldest typed message in the world. No one has yet succeeded in decoding the message or even working out what language it is written in. One scholar believes it is a list of soldiers, while others think it could describe how the Phaistos palace was constructed.

This clay tablet has cuneiform writing on it. It was made nearly 4,000 years ago in what is now northern Iraq.

pictures of things like trees, clouds, buffaloes, and mountains that could be combined to make messages. When stories were written in this way, the symbols were drawn so that they curved around in a circle instead of following the straight lines that people use today.

Picture writing uses symbols based on the meanings of words. Languages such as English work in a very different way. Instead of using pictures, they use written symbols to indicate the sounds of spoken letters and words. These, in turn, evoke meaningful ideas or mental pictures. When we read the word *table*, we say "tay-buhl" in our heads and think of a mental picture of a table. All written languages are based on the idea of writing down either

the meanings or the sounds of spoken languages; most languages mix both these approaches.

The first people to develop a written language were the Sumerians of Mesopotamia (now part of Iraq) about 3500 B.C.E. They gradually developed a system called cuneiform. This involved using a wedge-shaped stick to make marks in soft clay. The marks were ordered to make words and syllables (parts of words).

Several hundred years later, the ancient Egyptians developed a more advanced writing system known as hieroglyphics. It was based on hundreds of different picture symbols. The language used by Chinese people also uses picture symbols (pictograms) and was invented about 1800 B.C.E. For example, the Chinese word for chair is made up of the three pictograms that mean *person*, *tree*, and *sitting*. Within a few hundred years, Chinese had developed into a complex language with thousands of pictograms, most of which are still used today.

Modern written languages, such as English, evolved when ancient peoples, including the Phoenicians and Japanese, simplified earlier writing systems and started to write down the sounds of words instead of their meanings. The ancient Greeks devised the modern alphabet of vowels and consonants similar to our own. This system allows spoken words to be converted easily into written ones, and vice versa.

ALPHABETS

As this inscription on a Roman tablet shows, the alphabet we use today has not changed that much in the last 2,000 years.

Most people think of the alphabet as a collection of letters from which words can be assembled, but it is much more than this. An alphabet is what connects a written language to a spoken one: It allows written words to be read aloud and spoken words to be written down.

Alphabets developed when people started to write down symbols that represented the sound of a word instead of its meaning. The first alphabet was developed between 1700 and 1500 B.C.E. by the Semitic peoples who lived in the eastern Mediterranean, where

Lebanon, Israel, and Palestine are today. It was a mixture of the pictograms (picture symbols) used by the ancient Egyptians, and the wedge-shaped cuneiform marks used by the Sumerians. Another Mediterranean people, the Phoenicians, used a modified Semitic alphabet, which contained only consonants (hard sounds). By 800 B.C.E., the Greeks had added more sounds, including the five vowels: *a, e, i, o,* and *u*. This made a powerful writing system that soon spread throughout the Mediterranean. Among the people who used it were the Etruscans of northern Italy. The Etruscan alphabet eventually became the *a* to *z* Roman alphabet. As the Roman Empire expanded, this writing system spread throughout much of western Europe.

In Russia and the former Soviet republics, and in many eastern European countries, people use a different system known as the Cyrillic alphabet. This was developed from the Greek alphabet about 860 C.E. It has between 30 and 33 letters, depending on the country in which it is used. The extra letters match the different sounds spoken by people in the region.

In Africa, Asia, including the Middle East, many people use alphabets based on the ancient Aramaic one. Aramaic was the language used in the Middle East around 2,000 years ago. It was the language used by Jesus Christ and his early followers. Aramaic itself was based on the first Semitic alphabet. The alphabet used to write Hebrew and other Jewish languages is based on Aramaic, as are the many alphabets used in south Asia, such as Urdu and Hindi. Arabic is one Asian alphabet that is also used in parts of Africa. This alphabet was developed in the fifth century. It has 28 letters and is written from right to left.

Modern communication from email to text messaging still relies on alphabets such as these, but the picture-based writing systems of earlier times are still very much alive. Transportation hubs, such as airports and bus terminals, often include simple pictures on signs to direct people who might not understand written information.

People also use symbols as an easy way to communicate the way they feel. Messages sent on cell phones or by email sometimes combine punctuation marks to make pictures called smileys, or emoticons. A colon followed by a bracket may indicate happiness :) or sadness :(A semicolon followed by another bracket ;) indicates a wink.

A few of the symbols used in Egyptian writing. Although some symbols, known as phonograms, were used to represent sounds, Egyptian writing did not use vowels so we will never know how it was pronounced.

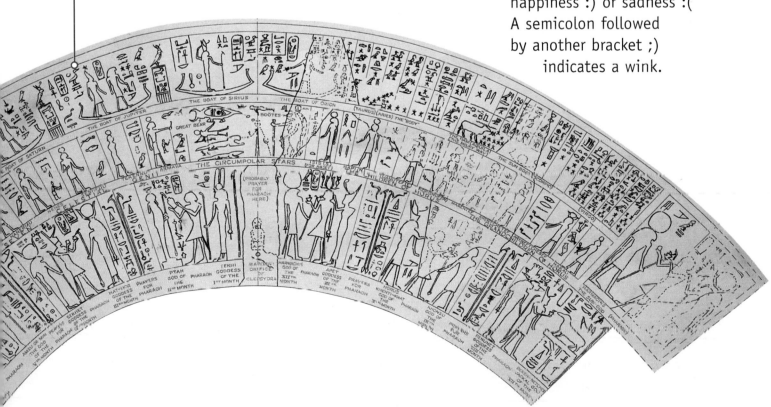

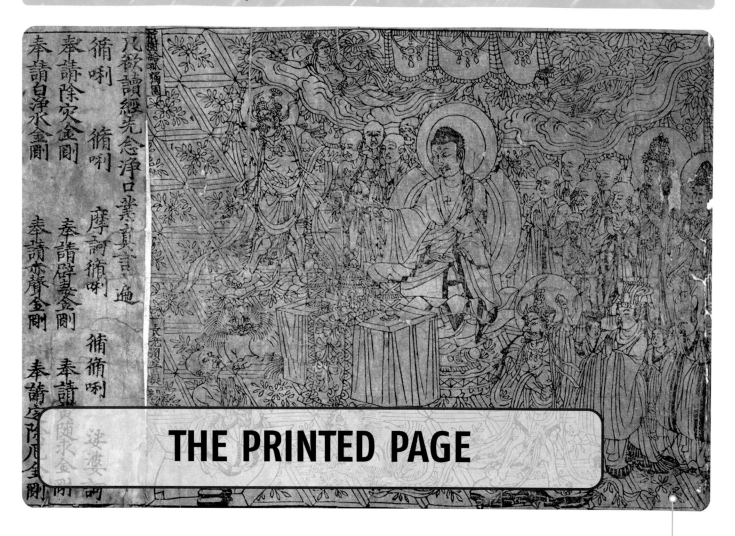

THE PRINTED PAGE

The Diamond Sutra *is the oldest printed book surviving today. It was made in China in 868 C.E.*

Writing started out as a simple means to record information. Copying this information so it could be used by someone else was a laborious process. For every, copy all the words had to be written out again. This job was done by professional copiers, or scribes. But the invention of printing made it possible to share information with many people.

THE FIRST BOOKS

Unlike the books we have today, the earliest books had just one long page made from papyrus, silk, or bamboo. This page was rolled up into a scroll. Ancient people wrote on scrolls using reed pens or hair brushes. The ink they used was made from soot mixed with vegetable gum. Once written, the finished page was rolled around sticks fastened to the top and bottom. Fully unrolled scrolls were about 30 feet (9.5 m) long; the longest scroll so far discovered measures 133 feet (40.5 m)— about the length of seven cars.

A much more convenient type of book known as a *codex*, the Latin word for "book," was invented in the 4th century. The first codices (the plural of *codex*) were wooden tablets covered with a thin layer of wax. Writing was scratched into the wax and could be erased if necessary. Gradually, the best features of scrolls and codices were combined. The first books were codices made from several sheets of parchment that were folded in the middle and stitched together. These were covered with sturdy wooden or leather boards. During the Middle Ages (5th to 15th centuries), few people could read or write. Books and other writings were luxury items until the invention of printing.

PRINTED BOOKS

Many people think a German printer called Johannes Gutenberg (1400–68) invented printing in the 15th century. In fact, the Chinese had invented printing more than 1,000 years earlier, and the process may date back even further still. Discoveries such as the Phaistos disk from Crete show that people were printing symbols into clay thousands of years ago.

Key inventions

Pens and Pencils

Modern pens evolved from quills. First used by the Romans in the 6th century B.C.E., quills were made from the central shaft of a bird's feather. This was sharpened into a nib and dipped in ink. Quills were replaced with metal-nibbed pens in the early 19th century. These worked in the same way as quills, but the metal nibs did not wear out as quickly as the feather.

The fountain pen was another 19th-century innovation. It was invented in 1884 by American insurance salesman Lewis Waterman (1837–1901), apparently so that people could sign his contracts more quickly. Fountain pens were easier to use than quills because they had their own built-in supply of ink, but they were still messy.

The ballpoint pen, or biro, is a more convenient pen. It was invented in 1938 by Hungarians Georg and Lazlo Biro. The ink used in biros was much thicker than in other pens, so it did not spill easily. Instead of a nib, the pen had a tiny ball made of metal that rolled a line of ink onto the page as the pen moved along. In those days, biros were sold for $12.50 each. Modern ballpoints (above) cost just a few cents. Early ballpoint pens remained quite messy until 1949, however, when U.S.

businessman Patrick Frawley, Jr. and chemist Fran Seech launched the revolutionary Papermate pen with its cleaner, quicker drying ink.

Fiber-tip pens were invented in Japan in 1962 by Yukio Horie, the founder of the Pentel company. They use liquid dyes instead of inks. When fiber-tips were crossed with ballpoints, the result was the rollerball pen, invented in Japan in 1973.

The earliest pencils were simple sticks of graphite (a soft form of carbon) used by the Chinese from about 200 B.C.E. onward. Harder pencils were invented in 1792 by French artist Jacques Conté (1755–1805). He mixed graphite powder with clay, cut it into strips, and then baked it. U.S. inventor William Monroe invented the modern pencil (below) in 1812 when he developed a process for covering Conté's graphite-clay sticks in cedar wood.

Printing began in China soon after the invention of paper in 105 C.E. The spread of religions such as Christianity and Islam encouraged the development of books in Europe and the Middle East. In much the same way, the spread of the Buddhist religion through East Asia increased the demand for copies of prayers and other religious documents.

To meet this demand, Chinese scribes began printing documents using wooden blocks into which they carved an entire page of text. They printed the pages by covering these blocks with ink and pressing them onto paper.

THE INVENTION OF TYPE

Although the Chinese invention of printing was a great step forward, it suffered a major drawback: Wooden blocks had to be carved for every single page of every book that needed to be printed.

A solution to this problem was developed in the 11th century. Printers began to cut up the large, page-sized blocks into tiny pieces each containing a single character. A new page could then be made simply by rearranging the wooden blocks, known as type, so they spelled the correct words. One set of blocks was used for many books. (*Continued on page 18.*)

This hard wooden cover of a Roman codex would have been filled with soft wax. Letters were written in the wax with the penlike stylus. The codex is folded in the middle like a modern book.

Typewriters

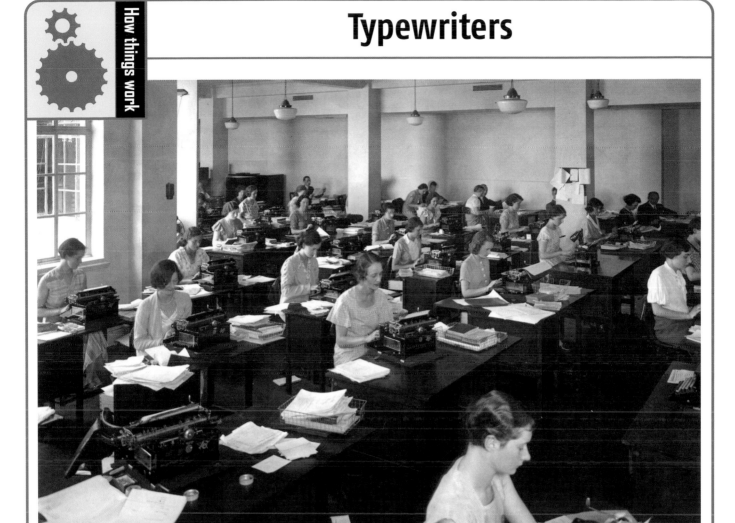

Borrowing the idea of metal type from printing presses, typewriters (above) made it possible for people to build up neatly printed pages of information, one letter at a time. A typewriter is made up of a keyboard, hammers with type at the end, a carriage, which holds the paper against a rubber roller and moves it from side to side, and a ribbon—a reel of fabric impregnated with ink.

Each key corresponds to a letter or punctuation mark. When a key is pressed, the corresponding hammer rises up toward the paper. At the same time, the ribbon rises upward. As the key strikes the paper, the ribbon is trapped between the type and the paper, making an impression of a letter on the page. When the key falls back to its original position, the carriage moves the paper one space to the left. This ensures that the next letter is typed beside the last, not on top. At the end of each line, the typist moved the carriage to the right to begin the next line. The paper was moved up a line using the roller in the carriage.

The typewriter was invented in 1868 by American journalist Christopher Latham Sholes (1819–90). People found they could type so quickly on his machine that the type hammers often jammed together, forcing the typist to stop work and disentangle them. Sholes solved this problem by rearranging the keyboard so the most frequently used keys were as far away from one another as possible. His QWERTY layout, named for the first line of keys, is still used on computer keyboards.

 Fact Typewriters have largely been replaced by computers. Word-processing programs do everything that a typewriter can, and a whole lot more!

GUTENBERG'S PRESS

German printer Johannes Gutenberg (1400–68) earned his place as the most famous person in the history of printing when he invented a press that used movable metal type. It formed the basis of printing technology for the next 500 years and is still widely regarded as one of the most far-reaching inventions of all time.

The pages Gutenberg printed were assembled from thousands of individual pieces of metal type, each one representing a single letter, that could be moved around and reused to print other pages. One of Gutenberg's most important

innovations was a method of casting identical-sized pieces of type using a mold. This involved carving mirror-images of letters into a piece of copper, filling these copper molds with molten iron, and then emptying out the solid pieces of type when the liquid metal had cooled down.

When Gutenberg had made enough type, he arranged it into lines in a wooden block known as a form, and swabbed the form with ink. Next, he placed a sheet of paper on top of the inked form and covered it with a mask called a frisket to protect it from stray ink. Then he slid the

In this artist's impression Gutenberg stands on the left holding a printed page. At the front a man is setting pieces of type into frames called composing sticks, and then setting these into frames to make page forms. The man sitting at the table inks a form for printing. Paper is placed on top of the inked form in the press, which presses a block (or platen) down onto the paper.

form and the frisket under the press itself. This was a modified screw press, similar to those used for making wine and olive oil since Roman

Gutenberg's *Bible*

This page is from the famous Gutenberg *Bible*, which was printed in about 1455 and is still regarded as a masterpiece of the printer's art. It was the first book to be printed in Europe and was written in Latin.

1. At that time, printed books were designed to mimic the handwritten versions produced by scribes, with ornate lettering and illuminations, or artworks.

2. Illuminations, such as this beautiful ornate capital letter were printed with a single piece of type.

3. Each letter of the Latin text was a separate piece of type. They are arranged in two columns of 42 lines each, so this book is sometimes called the *Forty-Two-Line Bible*.

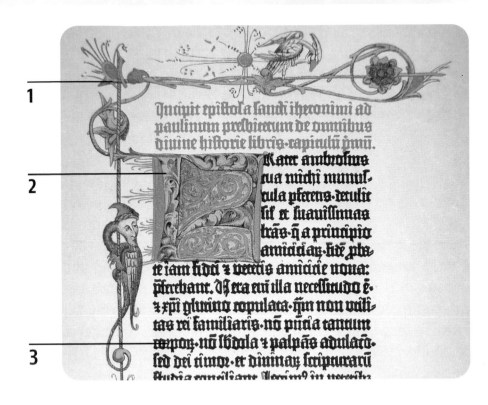

times. When the screw was tightened, it pushed down a thick wooden block called a platen. This forced the paper against the inked form and printed the page.

In 1455, Gutenberg used the press to print his most famous book, the Gutenberg *Bible*, which bears his name. This was the first complete book ever to have been printed with movable metal type. Almost 50 copies of this book still survive today, but only three of them are in perfect condition. They are kept for safety in the U.S. Library of Congress and the British and French national libraries.

Letterpress and Gravure

Simple presses can print from metal type in two different ways. If the shapes of the letters stand above the background, the printing they make is known as letterpress (1). Gutenberg's press used type like this. When ink is applied, it covers only the raised areas of type and leaves the surrounding area ink free.

The other method, known as gravure, is to dig the letter shapes into the metal (2). When the ink is applied, it fills the troughs created by the letter. The deeper the troughs, the more ink they hold, and the darker they print. Gravure is used to make much more richly printed pages.

1

2

Photocopying

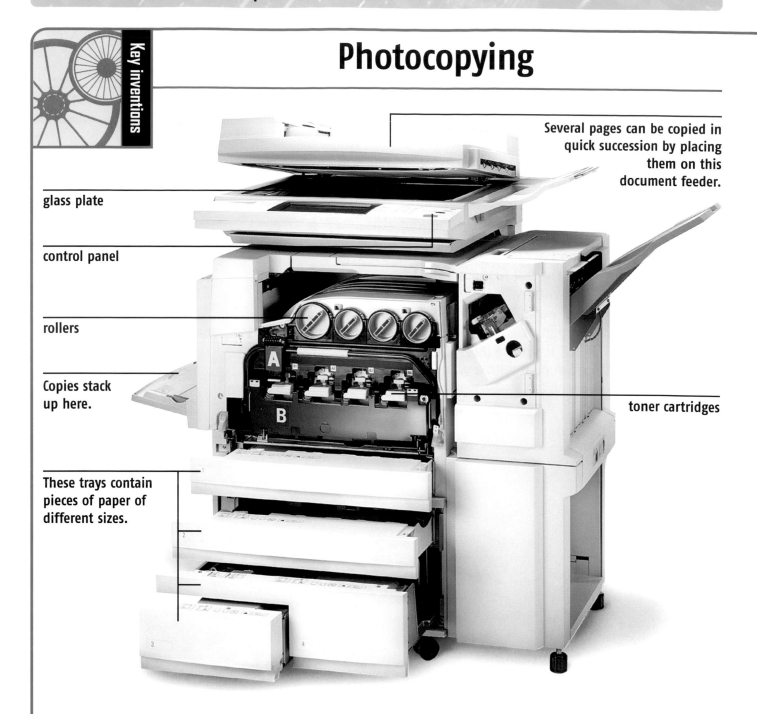

Several pages can be copied in quick succession by placing them on this document feeder.

glass plate

control panel

rollers

Copies stack up here.

toner cartridges

These trays contain pieces of paper of different sizes.

Photocopiers were invented in 1938 by U.S. patent clerk Chester Carlson (1906–68) and brought to the market 20 years later by the Xerox company. You make a photocopy by placing a document face down on a glass plate. When you press the "copy" button, a bright light scans across the document. The light reflects off the document onto a large metal drum that rotates underneath the glass plate. White parts of the document reflect most of the light, while dark parts absorb it. As a result, the pattern of light and dark is bounced off the document onto the drum. The drum starts off with a positive electrical charge spread evenly all over it. Where reflected light touches the drum, the electrical charge disappears. This leaves the drum charged up in a pattern that matches the dark areas of the original image. Powdered ink called toner is now applied to the drum and sticks only to the charged parts. When paper is pressed against the drum, the toner is transferred onto it. Finally, the paper is heated up to "fix" the toner and make a permanent copy of the original image.

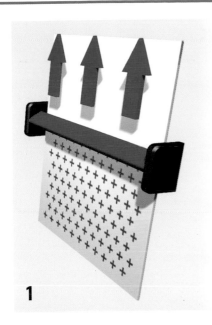

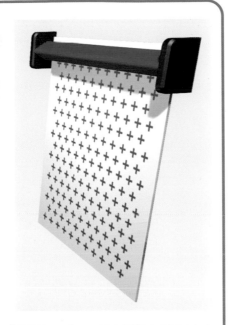

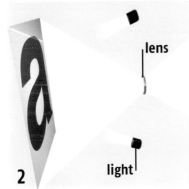

lens

light

charged area

3 toner

1. The surface of the drum is given a positive electric charge.

2. A reflected image of the document forms on the drum.

3. Toner clings to charged area.

4. The image is printed on paper.

5. The paper is heated up to dry the toner.

make it easier to lift the heavy platen away from the paper. Screws were replaced by levers early in the 19th century, which made the process quicker still.

The Industrial Revolution brought rotating presses driven by steam engines. The first of these was invented by German printer Friedrich Koenig in 1811. Instead of flat beds of type, rotary presses had the type curved around metal cylinders that could print pages onto continuous rolls of paper at very high speeds.

PRINTING TODAY

The idea of printing—pressing an inked surface against paper—has changed little since Gutenberg's time. One difference is in the way type is arranged, or set, on the page. Until the 1980s, it was still common to use pieces of metal type. Today, each page of a book or magazine is printed from a plate. This is a thin sheet of plastic (or another light material) that produces an entire page.

Plates are not built up a letter or line at a time from blocks of metal type, but created directly by computer using a photographic process called phototypesetting. Another innovation has been the development of small printers attached to personal computers. The fastest of these printers can reproduce an entire book, printed on both sides of the paper, in a matter of minutes—a considerable advance in technology since Gutenberg's day!

NEWSPAPERS

History is recorded in the pages of newspapers, and the history of newspapers dates back more than 2,000 years. Roman emperor Julius Caesar (100–44 B.C.E.) started what was probably the world's first newspaper in 59 B.C.E. Known as *Acta Diurna* (meaning "daily events"), it was written by hand every day and listed deaths, marriages, executions, and social events. The Chinese published the first printed news sheet, *Dibao*, in the 8th century C.E. using carved wooden-blocks. These publications could not be produced in large numbers, so instead of being circulated, they were posted in public places for people to read.

After Gutenberg developed movable metal type, it was possible to make enough copies of a newspaper to sell them to customers. By the late 16th century, printed news sheets were being sold in Italy for one *gazetta*, a small coin used at the time. This is where the word *gazette*, which is often used to mean "newspaper," comes from.

The first newspaper to appear in North America, in 1690, was called *Publick Occurrences Both Foreign and Domestic*. By 1800, 20 daily newspapers were being published in the United States. Early newspapers carried little other than business news until 1833, when Benjamin Henry Day (1810–89) started to publish the *New York Sun*. This was the first U.S. newspaper to include popular news, such as crime stories and gossip.

> *Newspapers are a good source of news. They contain more stories than television news shows. Most also contain a range of views.*

A front page of the Boston Gazette from 1770. The newspaper lists the names of local merchants who were importing products from Britain, which ruled Boston and much of North America at the time. Many Americans were boycotting British products at the time in a protest against high taxes. This dispute eventually led to the American Revolution (1775–83).

During the 19th century, new technology improved newspapers in a variety of different ways. Steam-driven rotary presses made it possible to print newspapers in large numbers. Railroads and telegraph lines brought news from all over the country.

In 1884, the Linotype machine was patented by American Ottmar Mergenthaler (1854–99). This could cast a whole line of metal type at once, making the printing process much faster. Another 19th-century advance was news agencies. These were set up to distribute news to many different newspapers. Among the first news agencies were Reuters, established in 1851 in London by German-born publisher Paul Julius Reuter (1816–99), and Associated Press, which started in 1848.

When radio and television were invented early in the 20th century, they brought news to people's homes much more quickly. But newspapers did not die out. Many became tabloids. Newspapers of this format had smaller pages with large pictures. The development of the World Wide Web in the 1990s, prompted many newspapers and other news organizations to set up web sites.

An offset press prints a color newspaper. Pages are printed many times on a long roll of paper. They are then cut into individual pages and stacked in the correct order.

LONG-DISTANCE COMMUNICATION

Letters are sorted at a London post office at the beginning of the 19th century. This sort of work is now done by machine.

In the 21st century, it is possible to send messages from one side of the planet to the other in a matter of seconds using telephone, fax, or email. Before these modern forms of communication were invented, long-distance communication took very much longer.

EARLY COMMUNICATION

Without mechanical and electrical forms of communication, ancient peoples had to rely on slower and more primitive ways of sending information. Simple messages could be sent over long distances using drumbeats, smoke signals, beacons (fires lit on hilltops), or blasts on a horn. During the Middle Ages, people started using homing pigeons to carry small written messages in rings attached to their legs.

Until the electric telegraph was invented in the 19th century, the only truly reliable way of sending a message over a long distance was to carry it from one place to another. In the Persian Empire

24

around the 6th century B.C.E., the ruler Cyrus the Great used a team of horse riders to carry messages much like the athletes in a modern relay race. The Greeks sent runners on foot to carry information many miles. But people could carry messages only so fast and so far.

FROM MESSENGERS TO EXPRESS

Ancient emperors could afford to pay for their messages to be delivered, but it was not until the 19th century that most ordinary people enjoyed the same service. That was made possible by express services. These were systems of carrying messages and money over long distances. Railroad conductor William F. Farnden set up the world's first express company when he started carrying packages on weekly trips between Boston and New York City in 1839. One of his employees, Henry Wells (1805–78), joined forces with businessman William Fargo (1818–81) and went on to form the American Express company in 1850 and then the Wells Fargo express company in 1852. With a fleet of stagecoaches, Wells Fargo rapidly became the

People and society

The First Marathon

History's most famous messenger was a runner called Pheidippides (right). One of the most important battles in ancient Greek history took place on the coastal plain at Marathon in 490 B.C.E. As the battle raged, Pheidippides was sent to carry news of the fighting to the nearby city of Athens. He ran the 26 miles (42 km) so quickly that, when he arrived, he dropped down dead from exhaustion. Ever since that time, the word *marathon* has been used to describe a race over the same distance that Pheidippides ran.

most important carrier in the United States, taking over many other express companies, including the famous Pony Express in 1861. Express services became much less important after the expansion of railroads and telegraphs during the late 19th century.

MAIL SERVICES

The Romans set up the world's first comprehensive postal system. Using riders on horseback, they could send messages anywhere in their Mediterranean-based Empire in just a matter of days.

Mail has been one of the most important forms of communication in the United States since the country's first postal service was established in Massachusetts in 1639. It was not until 1789 that a full postal system was set up, with 75 post offices across the nation. There are roughly 38,000 post offices and 326,000 collection boxes in the United States today.

At first the cost of mailing a letter depended on how far it was going. Charging by weight made the mail service more popular. Another important innovation was the development of ZIP (Zoning Improvement Program) codes in 1963. Today, much of the world's mail is processed by computerized machines that can sort letters automatically by their ZIP codes.

Stagecoaches prepare to set out from the Wells Fargo express office in Virginia City, Nevada in 1866. As well as passengers, the coaches carried mail and money around the country.

Pony Express

Before the completion of transcontinental railroads and telegraphs in the 19th century, mail was carried mostly by stagecoach. But coaches traveling to the newly settled western states had difficulty driving through the desert and over the mountains, and they were often attacked by Native Americans.

One of America's most famous mail services, the Pony Express, was set up in 1860 to speed the delivery of mail between Missouri and California. A team of fast horses and ponies carried small items of mail in special saddlebags (above). Lightweight riders, often just teenaged boys, were used for added speed. They changed to fresh horses every 10 miles (16 km) or so and were expected to cover at least 75 miles (120 km) each day on the hazardous 1,965-mile (3,164-km) trail.

Although the Pony Express rapidly expanded to include 80 riders and about 450 horses, it lost a great deal of money. It was discontinued after only 18 months in operation when the Pacific Telegraph line was completed in October 1861.

★ Fact Pony Express riders carried bags that were hung over the saddle and held in place by the rider's weight. This meant riders could change horses in seconds.

Penny Black Stamps

Stamps first came into widespread use in 1840, when English schoolmaster Rowland Hill (1795–1879) suggested a reform of his country's postal prices. Hill figured out that most of the cost in mailing a letter came not from delivering it but from the difficulty of calculating how much to charge people for sending different-sized packets over different distances. Another problem was that mail carriers had to collect payment when letters were delivered, which greatly slowed them down.

Hill proposed a much-simplified system in which mail was charged by weight, instead of distance, and paid for in advance using stamps stuck to the front of letters and parcels. The first stamp of this kind, introduced on May 1, 1840, was known as a Penny Black (left), because it cost one British penny and featured a portrait of Queen Victoria on a black background.

The changes Hill made to the postal service were so successful that twice as much mail was sent in England in 1840 as in 1839. Within 20 years or so, stamps were being used throughout the world.

SIGNALS AND TELEGRAPHS

The word *telegraph* comes from the Greek words for "distance" and "writing." It was the Greeks who invented the idea of telegraph in 500 B.C.E., when they built high walls from which people could send signals using flaming torches. A few hundred years later, a Greek historian called Polybius (200–118 B.C.E.) devised a way of signaling letters of the whole alphabet between two places by holding out a pair of burning torches in different positions.

These ingenious systems, known as visual telegraphs, were forgotten about during the Middle Ages. But in 1792, a French physician called Claude Chappe (1763–1805) rediscovered the idea. He sent signals over a distance using a series of high wooden towers. Chappe's towers had movable wooden arms at the top, which could be fixed in different positions to send 192 different signals. As each tower received

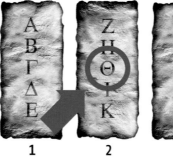   

1   2   3   4   5

This simple code was devised by a Greek named Polybius, more than 2,000 years ago. In this example, a signaler raises his right arm twice to indicate tablet 2. He then raise his left arm three times to indicate the third letter in that tablet.

28

a signal, it relayed it to the next one down the line. This system could transmit messages over many miles in a matter of a minutes. Chappe's signaling system was known as semaphore.

THE ELECTRIC TELEGRAPH

Telegraph became a much quicker and more powerful form of communication when inventors worked out how to send messages through electric wires. The first electric telegraph was invented in the middle of the 18th century by a Scotsman known only as C. M. His system used 26 different electric cables to send the different letters of the alphabet.

Cooke and Wheatstone's telegraph receiver did not use a code to spell out a message. Instead, electric pulses caused two of the five needles to point at a letter on the a diamond, spelling each word out.

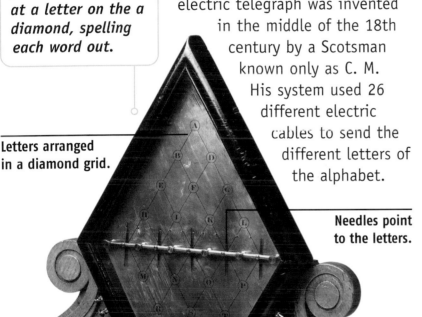

Letters arranged in a diamond grid.

Needles point to the letters.

keyboard

This design proved to be too cumbersome and expensive to install, and it never caught on.

A much better system was devised in 1837 by British inventors Charles Wheatstone (1802–75) and William Cooke (1806–79). It was based on electromagnetism, which had been discovered in 1819 by Danish physicist Hans Christian Oersted (1771–1851). Oersted had found that a burst of electric current could generate magnetism, which in turn could make a compass needle flick to one side. In the Cooke and Wheatstone telegraph, pulses of electricity were transmitted from a sending unit, down an electric cable, to a receiving unit. At the receiving end, the electricity was converted into magnetism that caused five needles to move in different ways. As the needles moved, they pointed to letters and numbers on a wooden panel and indicated the message being sent one letter at a time.

The Cooke and Wheatstone telegraph became popular in London, where it was used to send signals between railroad stations. But it was no match for a rival system, developed at the same time by American Samuel Morse (1791–1872). The Morse telegraph and the Morse code it used were carrying information around the world by the end of the 19th century. This marked the beginning of the modern communications revolution.

SAMUEL MORSE

Samuel Morse sends his first telegraph message from the Supreme Court in Washington, D.C., to his partner 40 miles (64 km) away in Baltimore.

On May 1, 1844 a rail locomotive steamed into Washington, D.C., from Baltimore carrying important news: The great statesman Henry Clay had decided to run for President. No one was surprised, because the same information had arrived 90 minutes earlier on the newly constructed Washington to Baltimore electric telegraph.

Constructed by the portrait artist Samuel Morse (1791–1872), this 40-mile (64-km) cable was the prototype for a system that revolutionized communication during the second half of the 19th century. Morse's telegraph sent and received messages using coded patterns of short and long electric pulses known as dots and dashes. The sender tapped out messages using a single key (similar to an oversized typewriter key). A few seconds later, a pattern of dots and dashes were printed out at the receiving end. It took more than a decade of experiments before Morse and his business partner Alfred Vail (1807–59) perfected the invention. Their efforts famously paid off on May 24, 1844, when Morse transmitted the first official Morse-code telegraph message to Vail: "What hath God wrought."

Within 20 years, most cities in the United States were linked with telegraph cables, many of which ran alongside the new railroad lines. The Morse telegraph was such an efficient way of sending messages that the idea soon spread throughout the world. Connecting countries together was the next step. In 1858, engineers tried—and failed—to lay a cable under the Atlantic ocean to carry telegraph messages between Britain and America. It took another eight years for them to lay a cable successfully using the largest ship of the day, the mighty *Great Eastern*.

Meanwhile, other inventors were trying to improve the basic technology of the Morse system, which could originally carry only one message at a time in only one direction. In 1874, Thomas Alva Edison (1847–1931) invented quadruplex telegraph, which could carry two messages in both directions on just one cable. Multiplex telegraphs, which could carry many messages both ways at the same time, appeared in 1915.

Telegraph Codes

In a simple visual telegraph, information is signaled between two places using flags or lights held in different positions. Morse's system of dots and dashes, known as International Morse Code (below), was adopted in 1851. Another signaling system, Baudot code, was invented in 1872 by Frenchman Jean-Maurice Émile Baudot (1845–1903). It used a pattern of five electric pulses to send messages between teleprinters (printing machines connected by telegraph).

Today, telegraph codes have been replaced by the American Standard Code for Information Interchange (ASCII), which was developed from Baudot code in 1966. ASCII is the code used to send text messages between computers across the Internet.

a	.-	h	....	o	---	v	...-
b	-...	i	..	p	.--.	w	.--
c	-.-.	j	.---	q	--.-	x	-..-
d	-..	k	-.-	r	.-.	y	-.--
e	.	l	.-..	s	...	z	--..
f	..-.	m	--	t	-	.	*dot*
g	--.	n	-.	u	..-	-	*dash*

The telegraph device used by Samuel Morse to send his first message. Pressing the key completed an electric circuit, sending a small current down a wire.

key

By the end of the 19th century, telegraph lines were buzzing dot–dash messages around the world. Although telephone and radio communication would eventually make it obsolete, the telegraph was the first high-speed international communication. It was very much the Internet of its day!

THE SPOKEN WORD

Telegraph was a great step forward, but it could transmit only a few words per minute. Another drawback was that messages could be sent and received only in places where there were telegraph cables. At the end of the 19th century, two new inventions solved both of these problems. Telephones made it possible to send people's voices rather than coded messages, while "wireless" radio could send sounds anywhere, with no cables at all.

TELEPHONE

Telephones send sound waves down electric wires. This was first proposed in 1854 by Frenchman Charles Bourseul (1829–1912).

Seven years later, German physicist Philip Reis (1834–74) produced a device that could send music down wires, although it could not transmit unrecorded speech.

February 14, 1876 was a big day in the history of communication. On this date, Scottish-born American inventor Alexander Graham Bell (1847–1922) and American inventor Elisha Gray (1835–1901) filed rival patents for devices that could send sound signals down electric cables: The telephone had been born.

Not everyone was impressed. When Bell offered his invention to the Western Union Telegraph Company, they refused to believe

An American family sits around its radio set in 1939. In the mid-20th century, listening to the radio was a very popular form of home entertainment.

Alexander Graham Bell makes the first telephone call from New York to Chicago, in 1892. In those early days, telephones had a separate mouthpiece and earpiece.

it would catch on and promptly turned him down. They were wrong. A decade after Bell filed his patent, there were 150,000 telephones in the United States and another 50,000 across the world.

One invention that added to the success of telephones was the invention of the switchboard. To make a call between telephones, there must be a cable connection between the two phones. It is not possible to have a wire running from every single phone to every other phone. Therefore, the phone is connected to a switchboard, where any phone can be connected to any other. The first switchboards were boards covered with wires and sockets. Callers asked an

How things work

Fax Machines

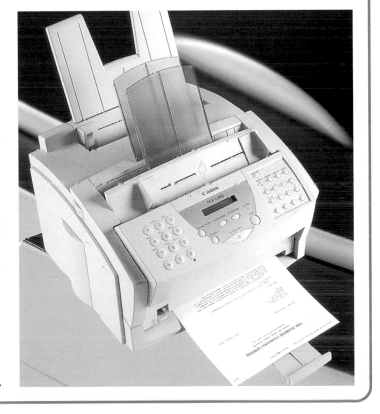

Fax, short for *facsimile* meaning "exact copy," is a way of sending and receiving documents using a telephone line. A scanner inside the machine stores an image of the black and white page as a long string of numbers. These are then transmitted down the telephone line to a fax machine at the other end. This decodes the numbers and prints the image onto paper (left).

Faxes only became common in the 1980s, but the idea is more than 150 years old. In 1843, Scottish philosopher Alexander Bain (1818–1903) figured out how to use a machine to send pictures over a telegraph line, but he never did. The forerunners of fax machines were teleprinters and telex machines, developed in the late 19th century, which could send text messages, but not pictures, over telegraph lines.

How things work

Tuning In To Radio

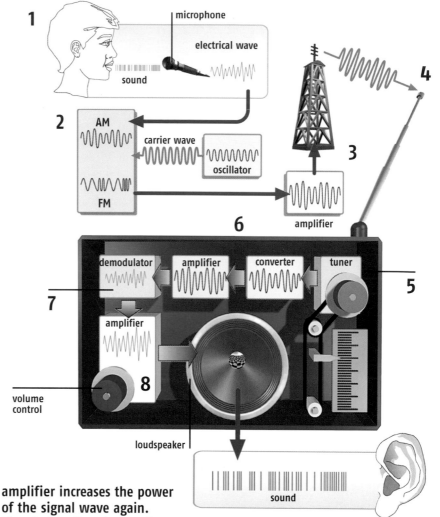

1. At a radio station, microphones turn sound waves into electrical waves, which make up the basic radio signal.

2. A device called an oscillator makes the radio carrier wave, which carries the radio signal through the air in one of two ways. In an AM (amplitude modulation) signal, the oscillator changes (or modulates) the height (or amplitude) of the wave. In an FM (frequency modulation) signal, the oscillator changes the frequency of the wave. Frequency is a measure of how many waves pass a point each second.

3. The modulated radio wave is amplified (increased in strength). The amplifier adds energy to the wave to do this.

4. A transmitting antenna beams the radio wave out through the air.

5. A radio set tuned to detect the correct frequency picks up the radio waves on its antenna.

6. A converter inside the radio changes the received waves to a lower frequency, while another amplifier increases the power of the signal wave again. Signals traveling from a distant transmitter will be very faint.

7. A device called the demodulator separates the carrier wave from the basic radio signal to make an electrical wave.

8. An amplifier increases the strength of this electrical wave so it is large enough to make a loudspeaker vibrate. This turns the electrical wave back into a sound wave you can hear.

operator to plug their phone into the socket connecting to the correct phone. Automatic electromagnetic switchboards, called exchanges, were invented in 1889 by Kansas City undertaker Almon B. Strowger. They were not widely used until the 1950s. Early exchanges could link 100 different telephone exchanges together; the latest exchanges can handle more than 100,000 lines at once.

Today, there are billions of telephones in use. Most are still connected to the local exchange by a pair of copper wires known

Wireless Telephone

Many telephones used in offices and homes are plugged in to the telephone network through a wire. Modern wireless telephones, however, make use of both telephone and radio technology so people can move freely while making telephone calls.

as a twisted pair. This technology has been largely replaced in other parts of the telephone network. Radio towers and satellites beam long-distance calls through space. Many telephone lines have been converted to fiber-optic cables. These carry telephone calls between exchanges as pulses of light.

RADIO

Radio must have seemed like magic when it was first invented because, unlike telephones and telegraphs, it transmits information without any cables at all. The science

1. The user can hear the caller's voice through a loudspeaker.

2. Information about the phone call is displayed on a screen.

3. A printed circuit board holds the phone's electronics.

4. A radio unit sends and receives signals to the base unit.

5. The user's voice is picked up by the microphone.

6. The base unit is connected to the telephone network by a wire.

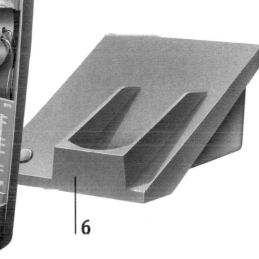

1

2

3

4

5

6

behind radio was discovered in 1864 by British physicist James Clerk Maxwell (1831–79). Maxwell suggested that energy was carried by electromagnetic waves. These are a little like waves on the sea but travel through space at the speed of light. About 20 years later, German Heinrich Hertz (1857–94) proved that Maxwell was right when he managed to produce electromagnetic waves.

British physicist Oliver Lodge (1851–1940) made another key breakthrough in 1894. He developed a device called a coherer, which could pick up the waves from the air. Italian Guglielmo Marconi (1874–1937) improved this invention and built the first practical radio transmitters and receivers.

Marconi's early radio apparatus was huge and cumbersome. It might never have caught on without the work of American engineer Lee De Forest (1873–1961). What made radios so big was the electronic components needed for detecting radio signals and amplifying them—increasing their strength so they could be heard. In 1906, De Forest developed a compact amplifying device called the vacuum tube. This made radios much smaller and more reliable. Four years later, he arranged the world's first scheduled broadcast from the Metropolitan Opera in New York City. With these two developments, radio became the chief form of entertainment in the 1950s.

GUGLIELMO MARCONI

The sound in the earpiece was faint but unmistakable. "Dot-dot-dot, dot-dot-dot." The man smiled as he made out the Morse code for the letter "S." It was 12.30 pm on December 2, 1901, and the man, a brilliant Italian physicist named Guglielmo Marconi, was standing on the blustery coast near St. John's, Newfoundland. The signal he had picked up in his earpiece had traveled 2,200 miles (3,500 km) by radio, all the way from a transmitter on the coast of Cornwall, England.

Many scientists had doubted that it was possible for radio to travel so far. If radio waves traveled in straight lines, they argued, surely Earth's rounded surface would mean long-distance radio signals moved off into space? Marconi's experiment proved them wrong. What he realized instinctively—and scientists later confirmed—was that radio waves can apparently "bend" their way around Earth. They do this by bouncing off a layer of the atmosphere known as the

Marconi spent many years testing how far he could send radio signals. He did much of this work aboard his yacht Elettra, above.

ionosphere, which works like a gigantic, invisible mirror wrapped around the planet.

Like many inventors before him and since, Marconi was used to having to fight for his ideas. Born to a wealthy Italian family in 1874, he failed to gain entrance to the University of Bologna and set about doing experiments of his own. At the age of 20, he read the obituary of the German physicist Heinrich Hertz, and realized that the radio waves Hertz had discovered might be used to transmit information. Using homemade equipment, Marconi carried out his own experiments and soon managed to transmit radio waves over a distance of 1.5 miles (2.4 km). The possibilities of radio were immediately apparent to him,

and he offered his invention to the Italian government. They turned him down.

In 1896, Marconi moved to England, where his ideas were better received. He promptly took out a patent on his new invention and, in 1897, formed a company to sell it. In 1899, he managed to transmit signals across the English Channel to France. He made the historic transatlantic transmission from Cornwall to Newfoundland two years later.

The British navy were among Marconi's first customers. Ships posed the ultimate communication problem, since they could not be linked together with cables. By the start of the

20th century, much of the world had eagerly adopted the new technology of telegraphs and telephones, but ships remained stuck in the past, sending signals over short ranges with lights and colored semaphore flags. All this changed in 1899, when three British warships were fitted with Marconi's new invention. Soon, every large ship in the fleet was carrying a radio.

Marconi's brilliant invention made him wealthy, and he received honors in the years that followed. Ironically, in 1909, the man who had once failed his university entrance examination won the greatest scientific award of all: the Nobel Prize for Physics.

Marconi with his radio equipment after the first transatlantic broadcast in 1901. He used Signal Hill in Newfoundland as his base.

CELL PHONES

An engineer installs a base station antenna. As well as voices, modern cell phones can send and receive videos (above right), emails, and text messages.

Cellular, or cell, phones send and receive telephone calls using radio waves. Unlike ordinary telephones, they are not connected by cables, so they can be carried around from place to place far from home, even from one country to another. This convenience has made cell phones the fastest growing forms of communication ever. There are now more than half a billion of them in use in at least 160 different countries.

Cell phones are so called because they use a cellular network. When you make a call on a cell phone, the phone sends a signal using radio waves to the nearest cell-phone base station. This is a device, usually within a few miles, that contains a radio transmitter and receiver, generally on top of a tall mast. Each base station deals with the calls in a certain area, called a cell. The base

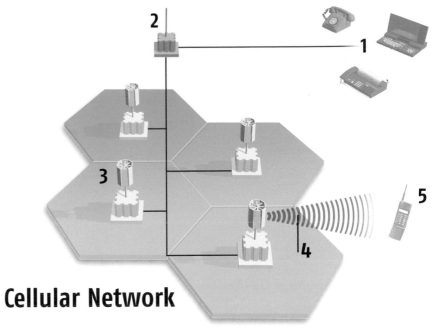

Cellular Network

In most networks not all cells are the same size. Those in crowded cities are smaller than ones covering open country.

1. A call made from a phone, fax, or computer travels through the main telephone network.

2. At a central exchange the call is directed to the cell network.

3. The central exchange's computer knows which cell

phones are communicating with which base station.

4. The call is transmitted into the cell occupied by the phone.

5. The cell's base station sends a radio signal to the cell phone.

station relays the call to a central exchange along a cable. The exchange moves the call on. This may be to the ordinary telephone network, servicing homes, or it may be to another cell network in another part of the country. When the call is answered, the person's voice passes back along the same path in the opposite direction

to the base station. Then the voice is sent as a radio signal back to your cell phone.

The cells of neighboring base stations overlap with each other. When you move from one cell to another, for example, as you make a call on a moving train, calls are automatically passed from one base station to the next without interruption. But if you move into an area where there are no cells, you cannot make or receive calls.

When you switch on your cell phone or move into an area inside a cellular network,

your phone immediately communicates by radio with the nearest base station. The computer at the central exchange then knows where you are and will route any calls you have to that cell.

Satphones (satellite phones) do not use a cellular network. They send and receive calls directly from satellites. They can be used anywhere on Earth—even in the middle of the Sahara desert or on top of Mount Everest! They may contain small cameras that are used to send pictures as well as just sound.

RECORDING SOUND

Since the gramophone was invented in the 1870s, a variety of different ways of recording and playing back sound have been developed. Modern sound recording techniques come very close to capturing all the excitement of a live performance.

MECHANICAL RECORDINGS

The celebrated American inventor Thomas Alva Edison (1847–1931) had done a great deal to improve the telegraph, with innovations such as a device that could automatically print out Morse code telegraph messages for

A replica of the first gramophone built by Emil Berliner. The listener had to turn the disk using a handle to hear the music.

A replica of the first sound-recording device, invented by Thomas Edison. Edison got the idea for this machine when he heard the sound his telegraph messaging machines made as they printed out Morse code at high speed.

stockbrokers. When the telephone was invented, Edison turned his attention to sound technology. He researched ways of recording telephone messages. The result was the Edison Talking Machine, invented in 1877. It consisted of a mouthpiece attached to a metal needle, which rested on a rotating cylinder covered in tinfoil.

When someone spoke into the mouthpiece, the energy in the sound waves made the needle vibrate up and down. This movement cut a groove of tiny bumps into the tinfoil. The sound could be played back by attaching a large funnel-shaped horn to the needle and running it through the groove. As the needle jumped up and down on the tiny bumps, a faint reproduction of the original sound crackled out from the horn.

SPINNING DISKS

Nothing like this invention had ever been seen—or heard—before. Some people refused to believe that this was sound recording at all. One scientist even thought Edison was a conman, and the sounds made by his machine were really coming from a hidden ventriloquist! Others, including German inventor Emil Berliner (1851–1929), could immediately see the potential of the new technology. A year after Edison invented his talking machine, Berliner came up with a much better sound-recording device called a gramophone. Like Edison, he used a needle that translated the mechanical energy in sound waves into a groove. But instead of using tin cylinders, Berliner used zinc platters covered with

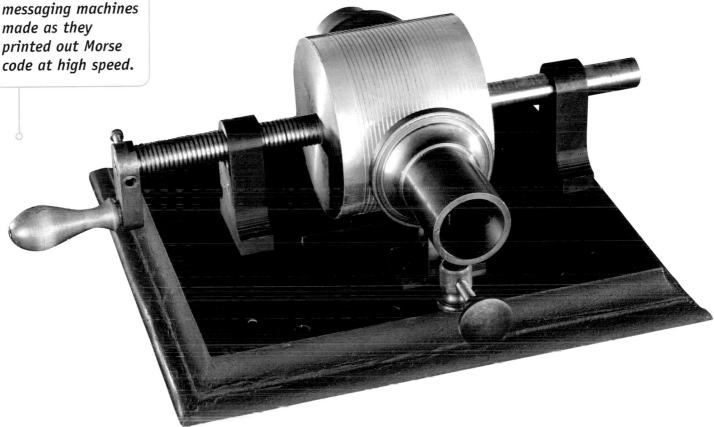

a thin layer of wax. A groove in the wax made the needle move from side to side. Berliner devised a way of copying recordings onto disks made from shellac, a material similar to plastic.

Gramophone records, as these disks became known, sounded better, lasted longer, and were much less expensive to reproduce than Edison's cylinders. By 1901, Berliner's Victor Talking Machine Company was selling disks from a collection of about 5,000 different gramophone recordings.

But these early recordings were not without their drawbacks. The main problem was that records could store only five minutes of sound. (A modern compact disk, by contrast, can hold about an hour of music). In 1948, the CBS record company introduced a larger record called a long player (LP), made from a lightweight plastic called vinyl. Unlike earlier records, which turned round at a speed of 78 revolutions per minute, LPs turned more slowly (33 rpm). They also had much narrower grooves, which meant they could store up to 30 minutes of music on each side.

MAGNETIC RECORDINGS

Gramophone records revolutionized the music industry by making it possible for people to listen to their favorite artists in the comfort of their own homes. But they were easily scratched and damaged, and the quality of the recorded sound was far from that

How things work

Vibrations

Sound is made when things vibrate. When you hit a drum (above), the skin bounces up and down extremely quickly. The vibrating skin pushes and pulls nearby air molecules back and forth. The vibrations in the air, or sound waves, rapidly spread out until they reach the air inside our ears. The waves make our eardrums vibrate. This vibration is interpreted by our brains as sound. Sound, then, is all about mechanical energy, and how it moves through air. Early sound-recording inventions, such as the gramophone, stored sound energy in a mechanical form with a vibrating needle. Modern sound-recording technology converts the mechanical energy in sound into an electrical form and stores this instead as a code.

of a live performance. Shortly after Edison and Berliner made the first mechanical recordings, other inventors started using electromagnetism in an attempt to record sound more faithfully.

Record Player

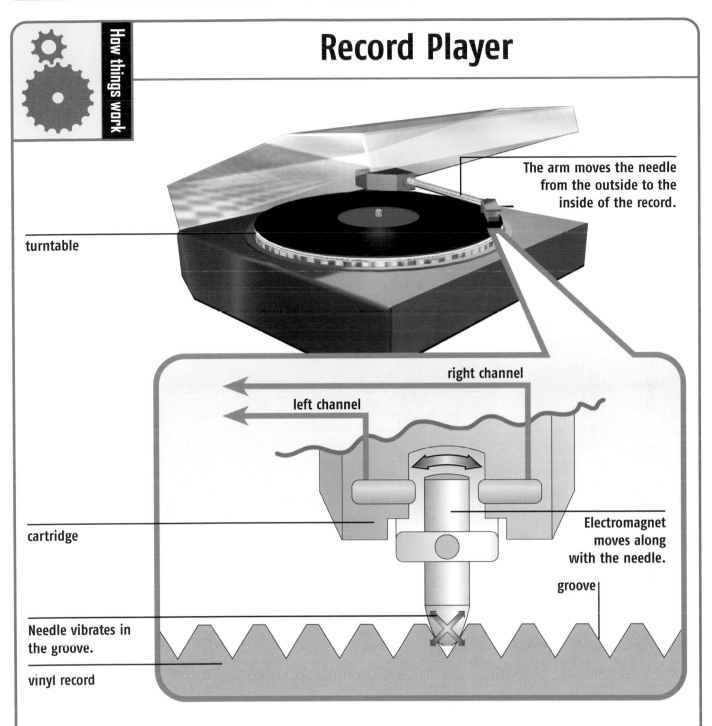

The arm moves the needle from the outside to the inside of the record.

turntable

right channel

left channel

cartridge

Electromagnet moves along with the needle.

groove

Needle vibrates in the groove.

vinyl record

A record player uses a needle to play back sounds from a vinyl disk, or record, that rotates beneath it on a turntable. The needle is a tiny piece of sapphire or diamond mounted in a small plastic cartridge. The needle slowly moves along a spiral groove from the edge of the record to the center. As it does so, the needle moves from side to side in minute zigzags in the groove. Inside the cartridge, an electromagnet converts the side-to-side vibrations of the needle into small electric currents. These currents are amplified and used to power the loudspeakers to produce sound. Modern long-play (LP) records have two channels of sound. Needle movements to the right encode sounds for the right speaker, while movements to the left do so for the left speaker. The needle senses movements in both directions and produces two different electric signals that operate separate speakers. This system produces rich, two-dimensional stereo sound.

Magnetic recordings are very different from mechanical ones. The sound carried by telephone wires and radios waves has been translated from mechanical waves into electrical ones by a microphone. Loudspeakers at the other end convert the electrical signals back into sound waves that can be heard. In making magnetic sound recordings, the electric current from microphones is used to control an electromagnet (a magnet operated by electricity). The electricity turns the magnet on and off, and the sound signal

Stereo Sound

How things work

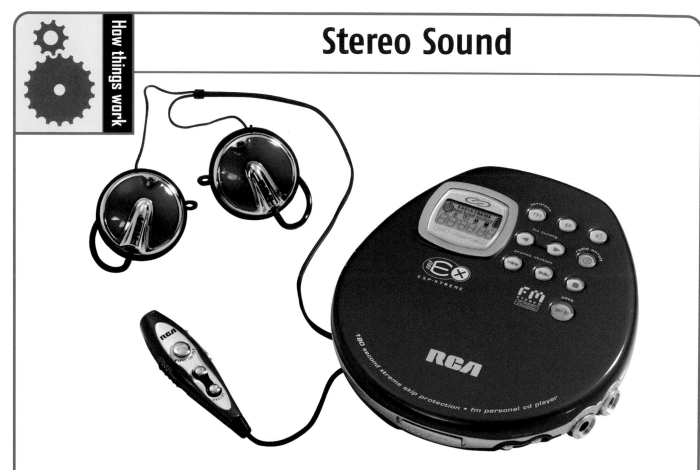

When we look out through our two eyes, different objects appear to be at different distances, and the world seems to flow around us as we move. In other words, two eyes help us understand the world in three dimensions.

In much the same way, our two ears help us hear the world in three dimensions, by allowing us to locate sounds in different places. Sound coming from the left arrives in our left ear before it reaches our right one. Our brain interprets this time delay, and so we not only hear the sound but know where it is coming from. Stereo recordings take advantage of this ability by playing different sounds into each ear. Our brains process the different sounds as if they were coming from all around us. This is especially effective when sound is heard through headphones (above). With headphones it is possible to make sound move through a listener's head or around the room.

Stereo sound is recorded in two tracks. The player decodes these tracks and directs each one to a single loudspeaker. Television surround sound is recorded in at least five tracks. One track supplies a signal to the television set's main loudspeaker, while the others are fed to speakers beside and even behind the listener.

is stored as a changing pattern of magnetism on a magnetic material, such as a cassette tape. The same process runs in reverse to play the sound back. Another magnet scans over the magnetized material and generates an electric current as it does so. This is fed into a loudspeaker that re-creates the original sound.

How things work

Microphone and Loudspeaker

Microphones make it possible to record sound by converting the mechanical energy of air waves into an electrical signal. Inside a microphone, sound waves hit a thin piece of plastic called a diaphragm and make it vibrate like the skin of a drum. The diaphragm pushes against a crystal. This crystal is piezoelectric; that is, it generates tiny pulses of electricity whenever something squeezes it. The crystal converts the diaphragm's vibrations into electrical signals. The pattern of electricity produced is then stored.

Loudspeakers work in almost exactly the opposite way to microphones. They convert the electrical energy produced from something like a compact disk (CD) into mechanical vibrations that create sound waves. Electrical signals from the CD are fed into a coil of wire. As they flow through the coil, they generate a changing magnetic field. This makes a piece of metal inside the coil move back and forth. The metal is glued to a large paper cone, which vibrates back and forth according to the pattern of electrical signals. The vibrating cone of a loudspeaker makes sound in much the same way as a vibrating drum skin does. Bigger cones, called woofers, make deeper sounds than smaller ones, known as tweeters.

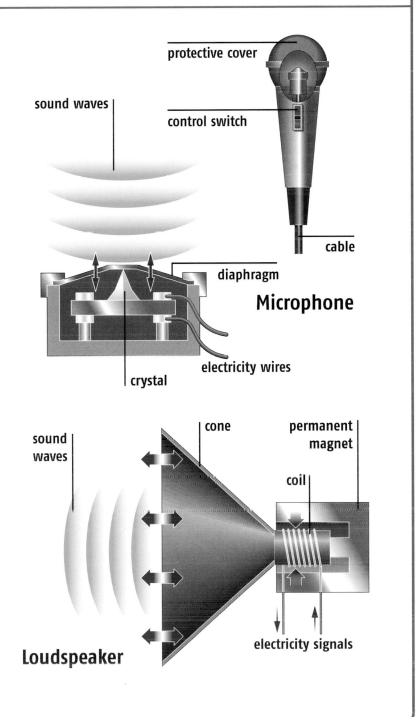

sound waves

protective cover

control switch

cable

diaphragm

Microphone

electricity wires

crystal

sound waves

cone

permanent magnet

coil

electricity signals

Loudspeaker

The first magnetic recordings were made in 1878 by American inventor Oberlin Smith (1840–1926), who recorded the sound coming down a telephone cable onto a length of steel wire. About ten years later, this very primitive telephone voicemail service was improved by Danish electrical engineer Valdemar Poulsen (1869–1942). His invention was the Telegraphone, a device that could record voices, including those coming down a telephone, onto a steel wire wrapped around a drum.

TAPE RECORDERS

Edison's cylinders had not been successful, and Poulsen's magnetic cylinders fared no better: They were too cumbersome and could not store much information. What was needed was a way of storing magnetic information in a more compact and convenient form. In 1888, Oberlin Smith thought up the idea of recording sound using a length of cloth coated with magnetized iron filings.

About 40 years later, German engineer Fritz Pfleumer (1897–1945) came up with a similar idea using a reel of paper tape coated with steel. The German AEG company spotted the potential of this invention and bought the patent. They then developed the magnetic tape as we know it today. This is made from thin plastic covered with magnetic iron-oxide powder. AEG began making its first tape recorder, the magnetophon, in 1935. This used

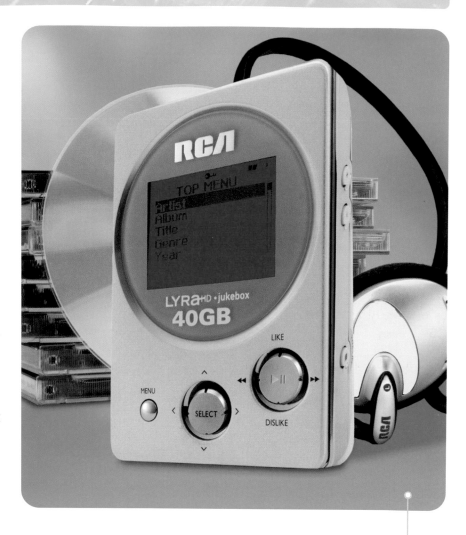

enormous lengths of tape on two large spools (or reels) that were mounted on top.

In 1964, the Philips company in Holland devised a way of packaging these reels inside small plastic cases. Cassettes, as these were known, became popular in the 1970s. They were so successful because people could use them to store their own sound recordings at home, as well as play back music bought in stores. They gained popularity in the 1980s when the founder of the Japanese Sony electronics company, Akio Morita (1921–99), thought up the Walkman, the first pocket-sized cassette player.

Digital sound recordings are now stored directly on computer chips. These are used in personal MP3 players, like the one above. MP3 files store high-quality music as a highly compressed code. Because MP3 files take up less memory than other types of recordings, they can be copied onto computers rapidly or sent by email.

Compact Disk

How things work

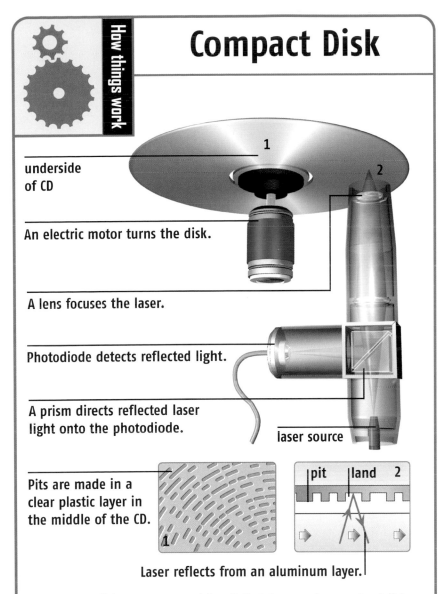

underside of CD

An electric motor turns the disk.

A lens focuses the laser.

Photodiode detects reflected light.

A prism directs reflected laser light onto the photodiode.

laser source

Pits are made in a clear plastic layer in the middle of the CD.

pit   land   2

Laser reflects from an aluminum layer.

A compact disk stores sound in digital form using an invisible pattern of depressions called pits. Inside a CD player, the disk spins at up to 500 revolutions per minute. As it does so, a tiny laser beam tracks across it, turning the bumps back into music.

Light from the laser is reflected in two different ways by the shiny aluminum coating on the disk. When the light hits a flat part of the disk, called a land, it bounces back into a lens positioned next to the laser. The lens focuses the laser light onto a light-detecting component called a photodiode. This generates a pulse of electricity. When the laser light hits a pit, it is scattered away. No light reaches the photodiode, so no electric pulse is generated.

As the laser tracks across the CD, the pattern of bumps on the disc is slowly translated into a series of electrical pulses. Electronic components inside the CD player treat the on-off pulses as a binary code, a pattern of 0s and 1s used in digital equipment. This code is used to recreate the original sound.

DIGITAL RECORDINGS

Record players read music from a pattern of bumps in the grooves of a vinyl LP; cassette tapes read it from a pattern of magnetized and unmagnetized areas on a tape. These technologies are known as analog, because the sound is produced directly from the pattern of information on the record or tape. Analog sound recording has now been superseded by digital technologies, which store and read music as a long string of numbers. Unlike LP records, which suffer from bumps and scratches, and tapes, which hiss and distort, digital recordings can produce sounds that are much closer to the original performance.

A number of different digital sound technologies are now used. Compact disks (CDs) and DVDs (Digital Versatile Disks) are like high-tech gramophone records played by lasers rather than needles. MiniDiscs are a cross between a computer floppy disks and a CD. They use both magnetism and lasers to store and retrieve data. DATs (Digital Audio Tapes) are similar to normal cassettes but store music at very high quality.

Music critics generally agree that these digital sound formats have many advantages over the analog formats they replaced. Indeed, many old recordings issued on shellac, vinyl record, or tape have now been "digitally remastered," or converted into a digital format. Often these sound even better than the originals!

ANALOG AND DIGITAL

Most people find it easier to tell the time from a digital clock than from the hands of an analog watch. "Analog" means that something can take any number of values. For example, the hands on an analog watch can be in any position as they sweep around the circular face, even between two numbers. "Digital" means something can take only certain fixed values: Each number on a digital watch can show only one of ten values, from zero to nine. As it counts the seconds, a digital watch will display each number for exactly one second before it changes to the next number, again for one second.

Early sound recordings, such as gramophone records or cassette tapes, used analog technology. Modern sound recording is mostly digital. It works by converting analog signals into coded strings of numbers.

ANALOG TO DIGITAL

Painting by numbers is a good example of how analog information can be converted into digital. Suppose you divide an oil painting into a grid of squares. Then choose

Digital Audio Tape

Modern Digital Audio Tape (DAT) cassettes look like small versions of regular analog tape cassettes. However, they record sound in a different way. Sound from a microphone is converted into electrical signals (1). This signal contains analog information, having a wavelike shape. Inside the DAT recorder's analog-digital converter (ADC), the electrical wave is sampled and turned into a binary code of 0s and 1s (2). Recording heads inside a drum then store this code on the surface of the magnetic tape (3). To play back a sound, the heads read the code from the magnetic pattern. The ADC then turns this code into an analog sound signal.

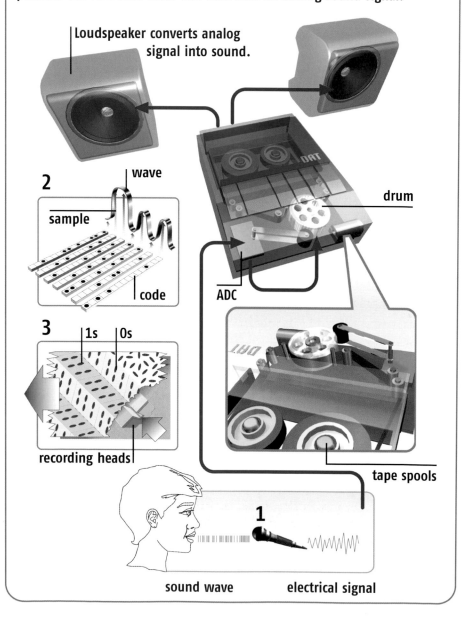

Loudspeaker converts analog signal into sound.

2 wave
sample
code

drum

ADC

3 1s 0s
recording heads

tape spools

1
sound wave   electrical signal

Analog Tape

Old-style cassette recorders use analog technology. Sound waves picked up by a microphone (1) generate an electrical signal. This signal operates an electromagnet known as the recording head pressed against the tape. The magnetic field produced by the head changes the position of iron particles on the tape making a record of the electric signal (2). Two different paths of particles store stereo sound in two separate tracks. During playback, another magnet, known as the playback head, reads the pattern of magnetic particles and generates an electrical signal. This powers the loudspeakers. The tape can be erased by magnetizing the particles so they all face in the same direction.

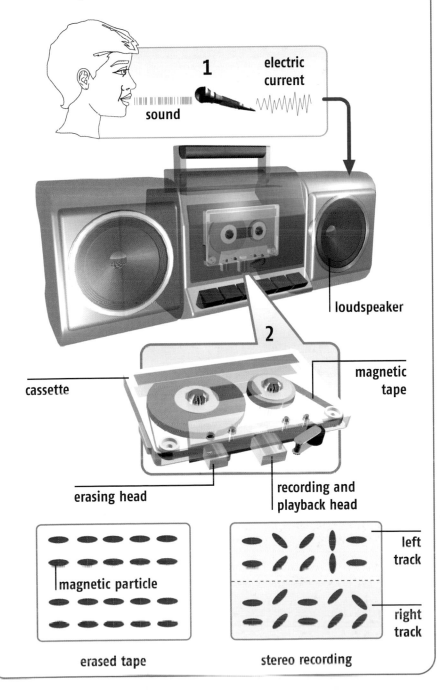

1

electric current

sound

loudspeaker

2

cassette

magnetic tape

erasing head

recording and playback head

magnetic particle

left track

right track

erased tape

stereo recording

one color for each square and assign a number to that color. Now suppose you read off the numbers for the whole grid in a continuous sequence. What you have done is convert the analog picture, which is made up of an infinite number of colors and shades, into a set of fixed numbers. This is what an analog to digital converter does with sound.

SAMPLING

How well the string of numbers represents the original picture depends on the size of each square. A grid with smaller squares, creates a more accurate conversion. It also generates more information, since there are more squares.

The process of dividing up continuous analog information into fixed amounts, such as describing a picture as a grid, is known as sampling. When music is recorded in a digital form, it is sampled about 48,000 times every second. In other words, 48,000 "snapshots" of the music are taken each second. While the actual sound may be rising or falling in pitch, the sampling process converts it into thousands of fixed tones. These tones are saved as a code of 1s and 0s. It is these numbers that are stored on a computer, or on the surface of a compact disk in the form of bumps and pits.

PHOTOGRAPHY

Some of the greatest moments in recent history have been captured in photographs. The basic principle of making images using light dates back about 2,500 years. Film photography is a 19th-century invention that uses light-sensitive chemicals. The latest photographic technology, digital photography, records images directly onto computer chips.

CAPTURING LIGHT

In the 4th century B.C.E. the *camera obscura* was invented in China. *Camera obscura* means "closed room" in Latin, and it was a darkened room with a tiny hole in one wall. Light from the outside world came through this hole and formed an image on the opposite wall. By the 11th century, Arab astronomers were using this technique to study the Sun without the bright light hurting their eyes.

The pioneers of photography in the late 18th and early 19th centuries used pinhole cameras. These were basically small, portable camera obscuras made from tightly sealed boxes. A light-sensitive paper or photographic plate was stuck to one of the

The world's first photograph, taken by Joseph Niépce in 1827. The image is of a view from the window of Niépce's country house.

The Science of Photography

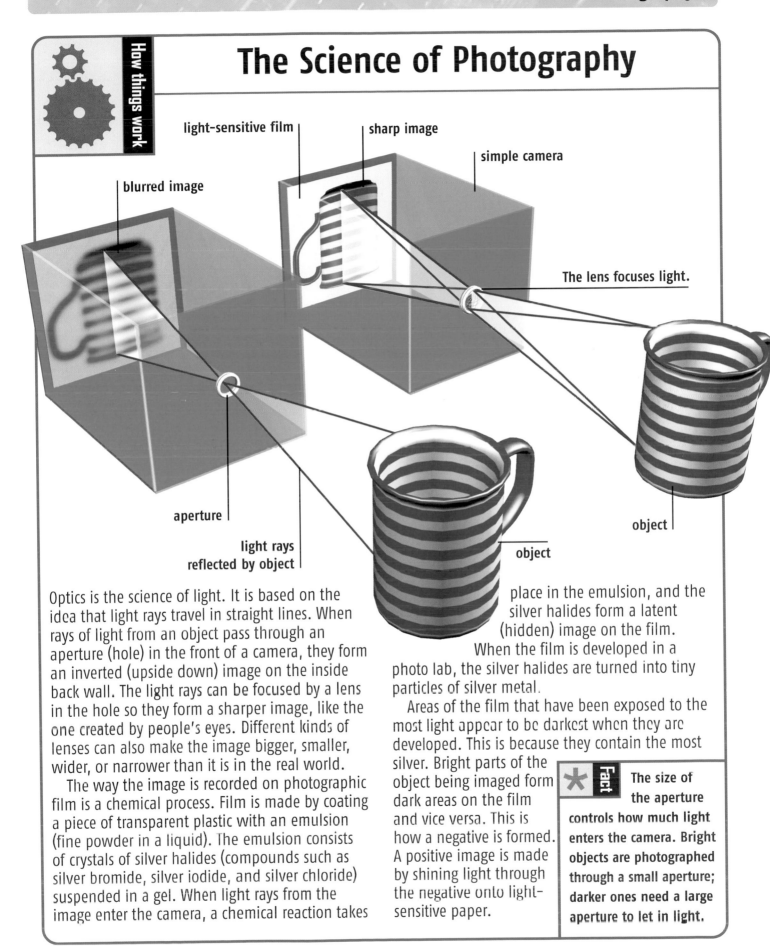

light-sensitive film

sharp image

simple camera

blurred image

The lens focuses light.

aperture

light rays reflected by object

object

object

Optics is the science of light. It is based on the idea that light rays travel in straight lines. When rays of light from an object pass through an aperture (hole) in the front of a camera, they form an inverted (upside down) image on the inside back wall. The light rays can be focused by a lens in the hole so they form a sharper image, like the one created by people's eyes. Different kinds of lenses can also make the image bigger, smaller, wider, or narrower than it is in the real world.

The way the image is recorded on photographic film is a chemical process. Film is made by coating a piece of transparent plastic with an emulsion (fine powder in a liquid). The emulsion consists of crystals of silver halides (compounds such as silver bromide, silver iodide, and silver chloride) suspended in a gel. When light rays from the image enter the camera, a chemical reaction takes place in the emulsion, and the silver halides form a latent (hidden) image on the film.

When the film is developed in a photo lab, the silver halides are turned into tiny particles of silver metal.

Areas of the film that have been exposed to the most light appear to be darkest when they are developed. This is because they contain the most silver. Bright parts of the object being imaged form dark areas on the film and vice versa. This is how a negative is formed. A positive image is made by shining light through the negative onto light-sensitive paper.

Fact The size of the aperture controls how much light enters the camera. Bright objects are photographed through a small aperture; darker ones need a large aperture to let in light.

inside walls and a tiny hole was punched in the opposite side. The light that got through the hole formed a clear image on the film.

Photography means "writing with light" in Greek. It was pioneered toward the end of the 18th century by English scientists Thomas Wedgewood (1771–1805) and Humphry Davy (1778–1829). They made images on specially treated paper coated with a light-sensitive chemical called silver chloride. Unfortunately, these early photographs were not permanent. Since the paper they were on was still sensitive to light, the images soon became

Key inventions

Digital Cameras

Instead of using photographic film, digital cameras record an image using a light-sensitive electronic device called a charge-coupled display (CCD). This works a bit like a television screen in reverse. A television makes a picture by lighting up thousands of tiny colored squares (pixels). In a digital camera (above), light rays from the object being photographed hit the CCD, which turns them into a patchwork of millions of tiny colored pixels. The camera measures the brightness and color of the light in each pixel and turns this information into a code. In this way, a picture becomes a long series of numbers, a digital picture, that a computer can store or print.

Many people use disposable cameras. These come with film already loaded. Once the film is finished, the whole camera is taken back to the store for development.

(allowed light onto it) for about eight hours, until a ghostly white image formed. The main drawback of Niépce's method was the very long exposure time. Imagine having to sit still for eight hours to have your photograph taken!

DAGUERRE AND FOX TALBOT

After Niépce's death, a better method was invented by his partner, French painter Louis Daguerre (1787–1851). This was the daguerreotype, a kind of photography that produced sharp, detailed images. To take a daguerreotype, silver plates coated with silver iodide were exposed inside a camera for just a few minutes. Then the exposed plates were heated up with mercury vapor to make the final image appear on the metal.

Daguerre made his invention in 1839. The same year, English inventor William Henry Fox Talbot (1800–77) developed a rival process for taking photos. He used a light-sensitive paper to produce a negative photographic image. Negative images are ones where light areas appear dark and dark ones are light, a little like an X-ray picture. Later, the negative image was "developed" into a positive one, with the light and dark areas shown correctly. Unlike daguerreotypes, which produced only one copy, the advantage of Talbot's invention was that many positive prints could be made from a single negative. But it still had two main drawbacks:

clouded. The entire piece of paper eventually turned black unless it was stored in a dark place.

Most photographic methods devised since then work on the same principle and use certain silver-based compounds that turn black when light shines on them. The oldest surviving photograph is a view from the window of a house in France, which was made in 1827 by French physicist Joseph Niépce (1765–1833).

Niépce made a photographic plate, which was an early version of photographic film, by covering a square piece of pewter metal with bitumen tar. He put the plate inside a simple camera, exposed it

SLR Camera

The single-lens reflex (SLR) camera is used by most professional photographers because it allows them to see the same image as the one captured on film.

1. Light enters the camera through a curved glass lens. Most SLR cameras work with several interchangeable lenses. Each lens is designed for a different purpose.

2. An adjustable diaphragm controls the size of the aperture (light hole).

3. The light entering the camera reflects off a mirror when the shutter is closed.

4. A prism directs the reflected light through the viewfinder, so the photographer can see the exact image entering the camera.

5. The shutter is between the mirror and the film. When the shutter release is pressed, the mirror swings up and the shutter opens. The light entering the camera can then form an image on the film.

6. This dial changes the shutter speed and controls how much light gets on to the film.

7. After a photograph has been taken, the film is wound on here. This pulls a new piece of film behind the shutter.

The photographic paper had to be exposed for several minutes, and it produced fuzzy pictures.

PHOTOGRAPHIC FILM

These problems were solved in 1851 by English sculptor and photographer Frederick Scott Archer (1813–57). Instead of photographic paper, Archer used wet plates to produce sharper pictures with exposure times of just a few seconds. These plates were made from glass and covered in chemicals that were still wet. Unfortunately, this process was messy and inconvenient because the wet plates had to be developed immediately before the chemicals on them dried.

What photographers needed were dry plates that could still be developed a long time after they had been exposed. In the 1870s, British physician Richard Maddox (1816–1902) invented the dry plate by coating one of Archer's wet plates with a layer of gelatin, a gel made from animal protein. It was soon possible to take photographs with exposures of less than 0.04 of a second, a million times faster than the photos taken by Joseph Niépce.

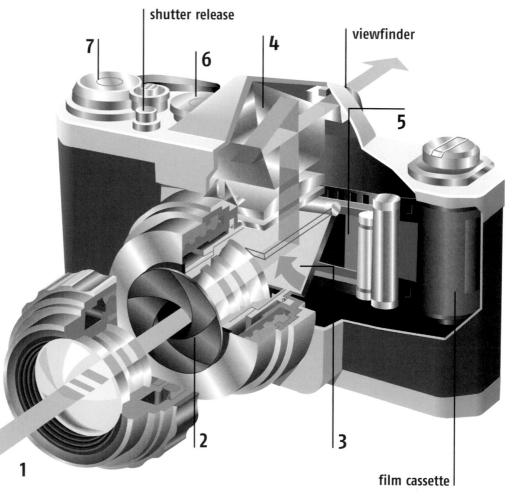

shutter release

7

6

4

viewfinder

5

1

2

3

film cassette

Photographic plates became obsolete in 1883, when American George Eastman (1854–1932) found a way of coating paper with light-sensitive chemicals. A few years later, Eastman began to use a strip of flexible, transparent plastic instead of paper. Wrapped up into a long spool, this became the roll of photographic film similar to those still used in many cameras today.

THE EVOLUTION OF CAMERAS

Photography remained a very specialized occupation until 1888. Then George Eastman launched his mass-market Kodak No. 1 camera with the slogan: "You push the button, and we do the rest." The camera was fitted with one of Eastman's film rolls, and customers simply returned the whole camera to the factory where the film was removed and developed for them. Easy to use and inexpensive, Kodak cameras turned photography into a hobby for millions of people.

Precision cameras that used standard-sized 35-mm (0.14-inch) film first appeared in the 1920s. Another advance came in 1937, when the German Ihagee company produced the first single lens reflex (SLR) camera. Until then cameras had two separate lenses: The viewfinder was for looking at the subject, and the main camera lens was for collecting light from the subject. This means the picture you see through the viewfinder is slightly different from the one that appears on the photograph.

With an SLR camera, however, there is only one lens for both composing and taking photos. You look directly through the lens using an ingenious hinged mirror that works like a periscope. When the shutter is closed, the mirror allows the photographer to look through the lens. When she or he takes the photo, the shutter clicks opens, letting light in; the hinged mirror flips up out of the way; and the light exposes the film.

The next step in convenience cameras was invented in 1947 by American Edwin Land (1909–91). The Polaroid camera automatically developed its own photographs, and produced finished prints in less than a minute. A color version of the camera appeared in 1963. Today, more and more people are taking instant photographs of a different kind, using computerized digital cameras.

This is the world's smallest instant camera. Its film develops itself, so printed pictures can be viewed just minutes after they have been taken.

MAKING IMAGES

"How charming it would be if it were possible to cause these natural images to imprint themselves durably and remain fixed on the paper!" This was the thought that came to William Henry Fox Talbot as he sketched Italian lakes in 1833.

Back at Laycock Abbey, Fox Talbot's grand English house, he set about experimenting. He made a photographic film by coating a piece of writing paper with silver iodide. Immediately before taking a photo, he washed the paper with silver nitrate and gallic acid. He then placed the still-moist paper inside his camera and made a picture by exposing the paper to light for about a minute. This made the negative image from which Fox Talbot later printed the final positive image. The oldest surviving negative is at the library at Laycock Abbey in 1835.

Producing a finished photographic negative is called developing. Making a positive print from a negative is called printing. Although developing and printing are somewhat more advanced now, they are still based on

A photograph of trees reflecting in a lake taken by William Fox Talbot in 1843. These early images were called talbotypes.

Modern photoprocessors display images on a screen before printing. This allows blemishes such as "red-eye" to be removed first.

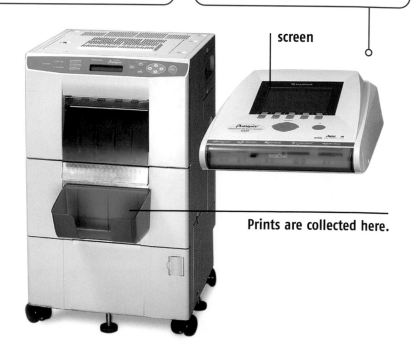

screen

Prints are collected here.

Developing and Printing

Films must be developed inside a dark room (below right), where no light can damage the exposed film. The process of turning the film into printed pictures involves several stages:

Developing: The film is bathed in a liquid called developer. This starts a chemical reaction that changes the silver halide particles in the film into metallic silver crystals.

Stopping: Once the film is developed enough, it is placed in a "stop bath," which contains acid and water. This halts the developing process and prevents the film from turning totally black.

Fixing: The film is rinsed in a chemical called a fixer to dissolve any unwanted silver chemicals. This hardens the emulsion and stops it from scratching.

Rinsing: The film is washed to remove any unwanted chemicals. This makes the final photographic negative.

Printing: Positive prints are made by shining light through the negative onto light-sensitive paper. Dark areas in the negative block the light creating white areas on the positive print.

the method Talbot developed in the 19th century. The photoprocessing machines in film outlets automate the whole process: You simply drop the film in one end and collect the printed photographs from the other end a few minutes later.

As well as developing and printing ordinary films, the modern photo-processing machines can also print photographs from digital cameras. Instead of printing films directly, images are scanned and stored by a computer. An operator can check these on a screen and edit them in various ways. Once the pictures are ready, laser beams "paint" them onto photographic paper.

MOVING PICTURES

When our eyes look at many slightly different pictures, one after another in quick succession, our brains are fooled into thinking we are seeing a single, moving picture. This is the basic idea behind movies, television, and video games that have dominated the entertainment industry since the early 20th century.

PICTURES ON THE MOVE

Inventors first found ways of animating a series of still pictures in the middle of the 19th century. In 1832, a Belgian named Joseph Plateau (1801–83) invented the phenakistoscope, which animated a series of pictures on the surface of a spinning cardboard disk. The better known zoetrope worked in a similar way. This displayed color pictures on the inside of a drum. Both these inventions used drawn images instead of photos, so they were really the world's first animated cartoons.

Other inventors tried to animate photographs taken from real life. One of these was American Eadweard Muybridge (1830–1904), who became famous for taking time-lapsed photographs of men and animals in different stages of movement. In 1877, Muybridge used 24 cameras arranged in a

A cameraman checks his view as a movie director discusses a scene with an actress. While most modern electronics are often getting smaller, movie cameras have stayed the same size. This is because they need to use a large-sized film to produce a picture clear enough for big movie screens.

line to take photographs of a horse as it galloped along. This experiment gave the first conclusive proof that galloping horses do, sometimes, lift all their hooves off the ground.

Zoetrope

Back in the 1830s, if you wanted to look at moving pictures, you did not go to the movies. Instead you all gathered around a zoetrope (above). This had a series of slightly different drawings on a large roll of paper that was wrapped around the inside of a drum. Higher up the drum was a series of slits. If you rotated the drum and looked through the slits, you could see the still pictures come to life. Other machines that worked in a similar way included the phenakistoscope, which used a rotating disk, and the praxinoscope, which was similar to the zoetrope but had mirrors fitted inside.

Muybridge had also almost invented the movie. What was needed, however, was not several cameras each taking one picture, but one camera taking many pictures over and over again. This breakthrough came in 1882 when French scientist Étienne-Jules Marey (1830–1904) invented a technique called chronophotography—short for chronological photography. Using a camera shaped like a rifle, he took up to 20 photos (or frames, as movie photos are known) per second of birds in flight.

THE INVENTION OF MOVIES

Marey made his early movies on light-sensitive paper, but this buckled easily and was far from perfect. When George Eastman started to manufacture sturdy celluloid film for photography in 1888, it was only a matter of time before someone adapted it for use in early movie cameras. That person was William Dickson (1860–1937), an assistant to Thomas Edison. Having studied the work of earlier pioneers, Dickson used their ideas to build a movie camera called the Kinetograph, in 1893. This used a strip of celluloid film with holes punched along its edge. A device adapted from a clock hauled the film through the camera using gears that hooked into the holes. The camera took 40 frames per second. These could be viewed by one person at a time through a projector called a Kinetoscope.

Within a year, Dickson and Edison were charging the residents of New York City 25¢ a ticket to view their Kinetoscope movies in peepshow parlors. When the Kinetoscope appeared in Paris, France, its success inspired two French brothers, Auguste Lumière (1862–1954) and Louis Lumière (1864–1948) to produce a better machine. This was called the cinématographe. It could project movies onto a wall. In December 1895, the Lumières opened the world's first movie theater.

MOVIE MARVELS

The quality of movie pictures has improved dramatically since then. Color pictures first appeared in 1906 with the Kinemacolor system, followed in 1922 by an improved system called Technicolor. Pictures also became bigger and wider with the use of different-sized, wide-screen projections known as Cinerama (invented 1952) and CinemaScope (invented 1953).

THE EARLY DAYS OF TELEVISION

In the 19th century very few people could watch moving pictures in their own homes, but the arrival of television soon changed that. Television is a combination of movies and radio: It uses radio waves to broadcast moving pictures through the air. Early television sets were very crude mechanical devices. Modern

IMAX movies are watched on screens eight stories high. The huge but very clear pictures are made using film which have frames that are much larger than regular movie frames.

Key inventions

Movie Sound Tracks

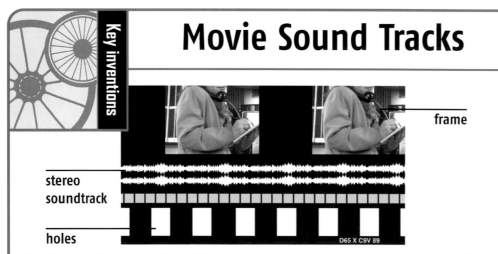

frame

stereo soundtrack

holes

D65 X C9V 89

The first movies were silent. The words characters spoke were written on the screen, and the action was accompanied by music. The first movie sound tracks appeared in 1926 with the vitaphone system. This used a separate phonograph recording played in time with the pictures. By 1931, film companies were recording sound tracks directly onto the film itself. A sound track is a squiggle-shaped clear area running beside the frames. When the film is being projected onto a screen, light shines through the sound track as well as the frames. The light is detected by a photocell. The light level varies as the sound track widens and narrows, and the photocell creates an electric signal which fluctuates in the same way. This signal controls the sound system in the movie theater.

television pictures are made with electronic technology, which produces clearer pictures.

The first television camera was invented in 1884 by German student Paul Nipkow (1860–1940). It consisted of a spinning disk with a series of holes cut into it in a spiral pattern. Nipkow placed a light-detecting photocell behind the disk and stood the object to be televised in front of it. As the disk rotated at high speed, the photocell detected flickers of light from the object. The cell then produced a corresponding fluctuating electric current. The current traveled down a wire to Nipkow's crude television set. This consisted of a single lightbulb, which was powered by the current from the photocell, and a second disk rotating exactly in step with the first. The fluctuating current made the lightbulb flicker on and off. When Nipkow looked at the bulb through the spinning holes of the second disk, he found he could see a crude picture of the original object.

This ingenious mechanical television was improved greatly by Scottish engineer John Logie Baird (1888–1946), who made the first television transmission of a moving picture in 1923. By 1928, he had broadcast television pictures of people's faces from London to New York. In the years that followed, Baird became an enthusiastic promoter of television technology. But the mechanical system he had developed from Nipkow's original invention soon became completely obsolete.

In its place came electronic television sets. They were inspired by the work of German physicist Karl Braun (1850–1919), who invented the electronic cathode-ray tube in 1897. This device makes a picture by scanning a beam of electrons (or cathode rays, as electrons used to be called) across a glass screen covered with white phosphor crystals. When the beam hits the phosphor, it makes a tiny glowing dot. As the beam scans back and forth, while switching on and off, it makes dots appear in some places and not in others. Many dots build up a complete image.

TELEVISION AGE

Modern television cameras first appeared in 1923, when Russian-born American engineer Vladimir Zworykin (1889–1982) invented the iconoscope. This device used thousands of photoelectric cells like Nipkow's "camera." These could turn an image into an on-off pattern of electric currents. A rival device known as an image dissector tube was invented shortly afterward by American Philo Farnsworth (1906–71).

Once the technology for television cameras and TVs had become available, television broadcasts soon followed. The first broadcasts were made by the British Broadcasting Company (BBC) in London, England, in 1927, and by RCA and NBC in the United States in 1930. Regular broadcasts, did not begin

In the 1950s, television took over from radio as the most popular form of family entertainment. Today there are 200 million TV sets in the United States alone.

TV Remote

Remote controls allow people to change channels without having to get up.

1. The remote sends signals as an infrared beam from this panel.

2. This remote uses touch-screen technology. Users select services displayed on the main screen.

3. As well as controlling the TV, this remote will also send signals to video, DVD, and music players.

This TV does not have a cathode-ray tube. Instead it has a flat screen that makes very clear pictures using liquid crystals.

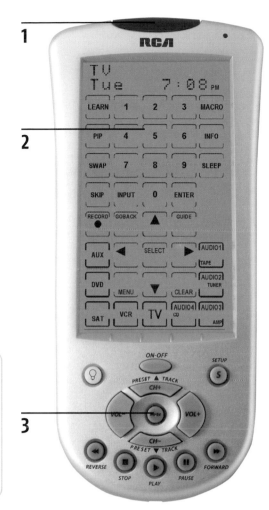

until the late 1940s. Color television made its first appearance in the 1950s.

TELEVISION TODAY

Television has come a long way since then, and improved forms of television have now appeared. High-definition television (HDTV) creates an image with twice as many lines of dots as on the screen of normal television. This produces a very clear picture.

Like other digital technology, television signals sent in binary code produce clearer images than analog ones. Digital television is also interactive. Viewers use the remote control to access extra information, respond to studio polls, and even choose their favorite camera angles, or select replays during sporting events.

STUDIO TO SET

Just as radio converts sound into an electric current, so television pictures are transmitted by turning them into electric signals with television cameras. These signals are sent through the air in the form of radio waves by transmitters on top of large antennas. The signals are received by the smaller antennas on people's homes, and turned back into pictures by television sets. Television is not always broadcast through the air. Cable TV is transmitted directly down a thick copper wire or fiber-optic cable. Satellite TV signals are beamed down from a communications satellite to a roof-top satellite dish.

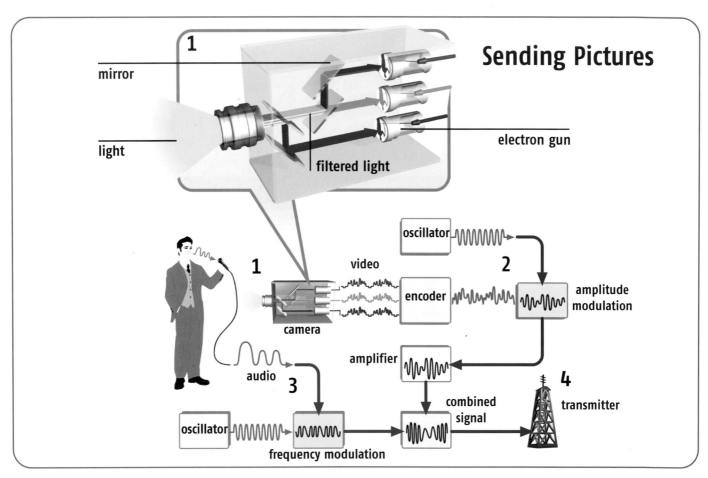

Sending Pictures

1. **Video signal:** Light enters the television camera. A system of mirrors and filters turns the picture into separate red, green, and blue images. Three electron guns scan beams over each image to produce video signals.
2. **Radio wave:** These signals are added to a regular radio carrier wave. The carrier wave is made by a device called an oscillator. The video signal is combined with the carrier wave by amplitude modulation (AM). This process changes the amplitude (size) of the wave. The AM wave is amplified before transmission.
3. **Audio signal:** Sound, or audio, signals from the person being televized are treated differently. They are added to the carrier wave by a different process called frequency modulation (FM). This changes the frequency of the carrier wave.
4. **Transmission:** The audio signal and the video signal are mixed together. They are then broadcast from a tall transmitting antenna.

Receiving Pictures

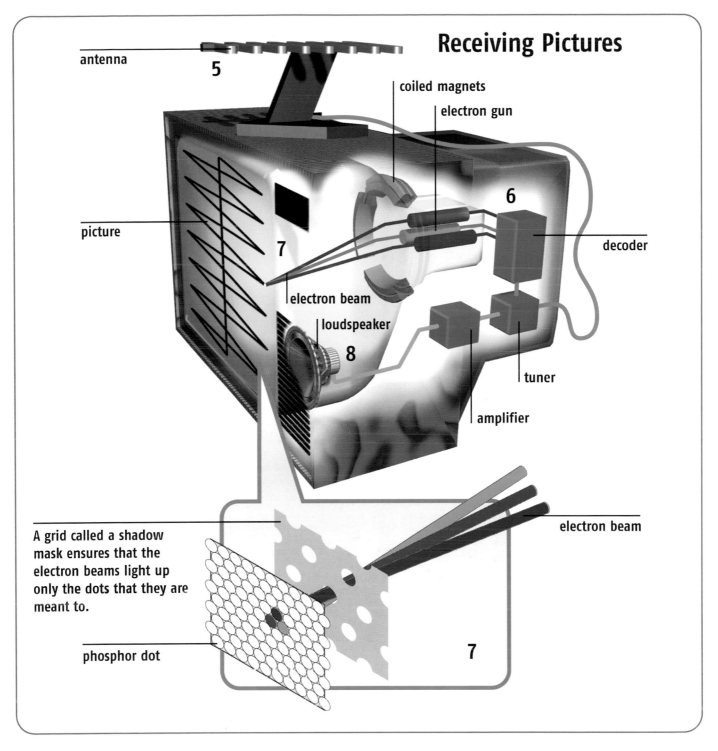

antenna

5

coiled magnets

electron gun

picture

6

decoder

7

electron beam

loudspeaker

8

tuner

amplifier

A grid called a shadow mask ensures that the electron beams light up only the dots that they are meant to.

electron beam

phosphor dot

7

5. Reception: The television's antenna picks up the signal sent by the transmitter antenna.
6. Decoding: The tuner selects a channel from the incoming signal. The decoder reads the video signal from the carrier wave and splits it into separate red, blue, and green video signals.

7. Electron beams: Each signal drives one of three electron guns that paint three colored pictures on the television screen. The electron guns produce beams of electrons (negatively charged particles) that can be positioned on the screen by magnets. The electron beams scan back and

forth over the screen lighting up crystals of phosphor. These dots of light make up the complete picture.
8. Sound signal: An amplifier increases the power of the audio signal. This is fed into a speaker, which produces sound in time with the television picture.

THE FIRST COMPUTERS

A full-sized replica of Charles Babbage's Difference Engine. Babbage's machines could perform calculations and remember the answers. They were the first computers.

The word *compute* means to figure out the results of a calculation, and computers can trace their history right back to the first calculating machine, the abacus, invented around 400 B.C.E. Mechanical calculators were invented in the 17th century. These used metal gears (toothed wheels) made to exact sizes. The first machine of this kind was invented by French mathematician Blaise Pascal (1623–62).

Although Pascal's calculator could do little more than add, it inspired other inventors to come up with better machines. Among them was German philosopher and mathematician Gottfried Leibniz (1646–1716), one of the most brilliant thinkers of his time. His gear-driven machine could add, subtract, multiply, and divide. It could also save the results of a calculation in a primitive memory device called a register. This was useful for feeding the result of one calculation into the next one. Computers still use registers to carry out basic operations today, although they are electronic rather than mechanical.

PROGRAMMABLE MACHINES

Pascal and Leibniz invented two of the basic parts of a computer: a calculator (or processor) and a memory. What sets a computer apart from a simple calculator is another essential component: A device that can accept a series of instructions, or program.

English math professor Charles Babbage (1791–1871) built the first programmable calculator in the 19th century. He developed a mechanical calculator in 1812 to help him figure out tide tables used by sailors. This was a task that needed a lot of very similar sums to be done over and over again. By the age of 30, Babbage had built a small prototype of a

Key inventions

Punched Cards

Modern computers read software (programs) off compact disks or download them from the Internet. But the first computers had to read their programs and data from small pieces of cardboard with holes punched into them. Punched cards like this were still widely used to program computers until the 1970s.

Punched cards were invented in 1801 by Frenchman Joseph-Marie Jacquard (1752–1834) as a way of controlling a textile loom. The Jacquard loom could weave intricate patterns in textiles using a completely automatic process, although the job of punching the cards (above) was very complex.

The idea of using punched cards was rediscovered in the 1880s by Herman Hollerith (1860–1929), who worked for the United States Census Bureau. Hollerith invented a calculator that could read census data from punched cards, making the job of calculating statistics much faster. By 1896, he had designed a calculator that could be used by many different businesses. His company eventually became International Business Machines (IBM), now the world's largest computer company.

calculating machine that he called the Difference Engine. He failed to complete the machine because he had difficulty making the several thousands of precisely machined metal gears that were needed.

With the help of his friend the Countess of Lovelace (1816–52), Babbage drew up plans for an even more ambitious calculator: the Analytical Engine. One of its key features was the ability to process information according to a series of prewritten instructions, or program. These would have been fed in to the machine with punched paper tape. The machine would have displayed the results of its calculations by punching holes in another tape.

The Analytical Engine would have been extremely powerful. It would have been able to carry out various calculations on numbers up to 50 digits long, taking one second to add two numbers and one minute to multiply them. But that power came at a heavy price. The machine would have been the size of a railroad locomotive and would have needed 50,000 metal gear wheels. In the end, as with the Difference Engine before it, the Analytical Engine proved too ambitious and expensive to build.

Although Babbage failed to build a complete version of either of his machines, he is regarded as the father of the computer because he was the first person to design a machine with all of a computer's key components: a memory, a processor, and a program.

People and society

First Programmer

If Charles Babbage devised the world's first programmable computer, his friend Augusta Ada King (1815–52), the Countess of Lovelace (above), was the first computer programmer. She was a distinguished mathematician who realized how Babbage's machine could be programmed in different ways by feeding in different kinds of instructions.

Since Babbage's time, computers have become much easier to program using simple computer languages, made up of ordinary English words and phrases, instead of the complicated instructions that were needed at first. Mathematician and U.S. naval officer Grace Murray Hopper (1906–92) was one of the first people to develop computer languages. She made popular the expression "bug" to describe an error that could stop a computer program. She got the idea from the way early computers used to malfunction when moths and other insects flew into the circuit boards.

CALCULATORS TO COMPUTERS

The transformation of calculators into computers began about 50 years after Babbage's death. Computing machines were still huge mechanical monsters at this point. During the 1920s, U.S. government scientist Vannevar Bush (1890–1974) developed the Differential Analyzer, the most complex mechanical calculator developed at the time.

Every calculator and computer made up to this point were analog machines. That is, they represented numbers in their memories as a position on a turning wheel or a store of electricity. In 1938, German engineer Konrad Zuse (1910–95) built the Z1, the world's first computer to use binary code. Zuse built this machine in his parents' living room using an elaborate mechanism of moving metal plates. Binary code represents numbers as strings of 1s and 0s. People normally count in decimals, using all ten units, from 0 to 9.

Although Zuse's machine was still a mechanical device, it was the first digital computer. Instead of representing data on an analog scale—the position along a scale, or the size of a stored electric charge—the Z1 represented the code of 1s and 0s with movable switches. Each switch had only

Computer pioneer Vannevar Bush (left of picture) with the Integraph. In 1935, he built this computer at the Massachusetts Institute of Technology.

Enormous ENIAC

The first significant modern computer was a monster of a machine. Known as the Electronic Numerical Integrator and Calculator (ENIAC), the machine (right, with designer John Mauchly) was 100 feet (24 m) long, about the same length as 100 laptop computers sitting side by side) and 8 feet (2.5 m) high. Inside were 18,000 vacuum tubes. Despite its size, ENIAC was thousands of times less powerful than today's PCs. However, at the time, ENIAC was about 1,000 times faster than anything made before. It could perform about 5,000 additions and 1,000 multiplications per second. The computer was reprogrammed to make new calculations by rearranging hundreds of wires and sockets.

Fact ENIAC needed a large amount of electricity to power its thousands of vacuum tubes. When it was calculating, it consumed 150 kilowatts. This is as much energy as 150 electric toasters working full time.

two possible positions. One position represented *0*, while the other stored a *1*. All computers now use this on–off system to store data.

The first electrical digital computer was built in 1944 at Harvard University by math expert Howard Aiken (1900–73). Known as the Harvard Mark I, it had 3,304 relays. Relays are switches that were opened and closed by electromagnetism.

Machines using relays were very slow. In 1946, scientists from the University of Pennsylvania, John Mauchly (1907–80) and J. Presper Eckert (1919–95), replaced relays with much faster electronic components called vacuum tubes. These had been invented in 1906 to amplify (enhance) radio and television signals. The machine that Mauchly and Eckert built was the Electronic Numerical Integrator and Calculator (ENIAC), the first general-purpose digital computer built from electronic components.

ENIAC was the fastest computer yet made. However, it took a very long time to reprogram because it had to be physically rewired. The first computer to be able to receive and store a program as well as data in its memory was the Manchester Mark I. This was programmed by Alan Turing (1912–54), a math professor at England's Manchester University. This machine was also the first to have a flexible random-access memory (RAM). The computer could access data in any part of this memory insstantaneously.

TRANSISTORS

Early electronic computers such as the ENIAC were absolutely enormous. Modern computers are small enough to hold in one hand. How did computers become so powerful and so tiny at the same time?

Each one of ENIAC's vacuum tubes took up about as much space as a person's thumb. Today, millions of electronic components that do the same job are packaged onto a microchip of silicon smaller than a fingernail.

The electronic revolution began at Bell Laboratories in New Jersey in December 1947. Two Bell physicists, John Bardeen (1908–91) and Walter Brattain (1902–87), invented a new electronic component called the transistor. Their manager William Shockley (1910–89) later improved the design. A transistor could amplify an electric current (make it more powerful) or act as a simple switch, like a vacuum tube. However, it was smaller, less expensive, and more reliable. Transistors were made from semiconductors.

These are materials such as germanium and silicon. They normally do not conduct electricity but can be made to conduct current if they are treated in certain ways.

Transistors were better than vacuum tubes, but they were still far from perfect. Computer circuits needed hundreds or thousands of transistors, and they remained intricate and difficult to assemble.

In 1958, an American engineer called Jack Kilby (born 1923), working for the Texas Instruments Company, figured out a solution to the problem. He realized he could shrink the size of electronic components by manufacturing them all on the surface of a piece of silicon. He had created an integrated circuit (IC). Robert Noyce (1927–90) of the Fairchild Semiconductor company made a similar breakthrough at the same time.

From the 1960s onward, it became possible to pack more and more components into integrated circuits and computers soon started shrinking. In 1968, Noyce and his colleague Gordon Moore (born 1929) set up a

company of their own called Integrated Electronics. Intel, as the company is better known, was asked to develop a range of computer chips for calculators in 1969. Instead of designing several chips, however, Intel engineer Ted Hoff (born 1937) invented one chip, named the Intel 4004, that would do all the different jobs. This was the world's first microchip computer or microprocessor. About the size of a fingernail, it contained 2,300 transistors, cost $200, and was about as powerful as ENIAC.

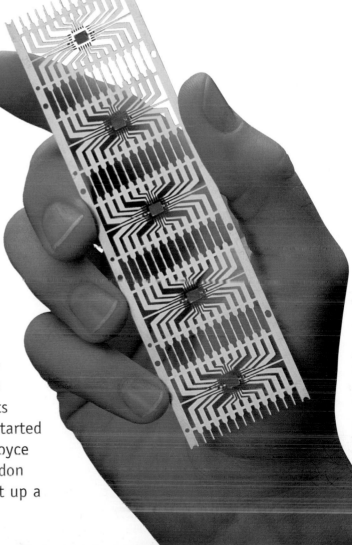

As this replica of the first transistor ever built shows (left), early models were considerably larger than those used in integrated circuits, or silicon chips used in modern electronics. This circuit board (right) holds five chips.

73

MODERN COMPUTERS

Fifty years ago, only large companies, government departments, and the military could afford massive machines like the ENIAC. Today, compact and powerful computers sit on most office desktops.

MAINFRAME COMPUTERS
In the 1940s, there were only a handful of computers in existence, most of them in universities or government laboratories. But people were busy developing machines that could be used by businesses. By 1951, International Business Machines, an American company now known as IBM, had launched its first general-purpose computer, the IBM 701. These machines used vacuum tubes like ENIAC. IBM rented nineteen IBM 701s to laboratories researching atomic power, government agencies, and large aircraft manufacturers, at $15,000 per month. The computers were used to process huge amounts of basic business data.

By 1965, companies such as IBM had installed about 25,000 computer systems across the

Computers are no longer ugly beige boxes that clutter desks with cables. The keyboard, mouse, and monitor of this computer communicate with each other using infrared waves, in the same way a remote control "talks" to a television.

United States. The most popular machine of this era was IBM's System 360. This was a suite of products that different types of customers could use in many different ways. This system was also the first IBM product to use integrated circuits.

Not everyone wanted—or could afford—these large computers, which were known as mainframes. Research scientists and other academics needed small computers for processing small amounts of data through complex calculations. IBM was focused on its mainframe business, so it was a rival company, Digital Equipment Corporation (DEC), which made the world's first minicomputer. The PDP-1, was put on sale in 1960. It cost

about $120,000—about one tenth the price of a larger but more powerful mainframe.

The trend toward smaller and more powerful computers continued throughout the 1960s and 1970s. The development of the first widely used microprocessor, the Intel 8080, in 1974 led to a new generation of computers that could sit on a desktop. The first of them was the Altair 8080, launched in 1975. Most of these complex machines were bought by electronics enthusiasts. That changed when two San Francisco computer hobbyists, Steve Jobs (born 1955) and Steve Wozniak (born 1950), started selling their Apple I computer at a cost of $666.66, in 1976.

In the early days of computing, huge mainframes were used to process large amounts of data. Most were used to perform simple calculations for businesses, such as reckoning the payroll.

A COMPUTERISED ELECTRONIC MUSIC STUDIO
by Peter Zinovieff

One year later, Jobs and Wozniak launched a much better desktop computer, the Apple II, packaged in a plastic case. The Apple II had a typewriter-like keyboard, used a domestic television as its screen, and read programs from an ordinary cassette tape player. With color graphics, sound, and plenty of software, the Apple II was the first successful home computer. It was an immediate success, especially with small businesses, and 50,000 of the machines were sold in the first two and a half years alone.

THE PERSONAL COMPUTER

Dozens of different microcomputers appeared in the late 1970s, but they were all very different from one another. One machine could

How things work

LCD Screen

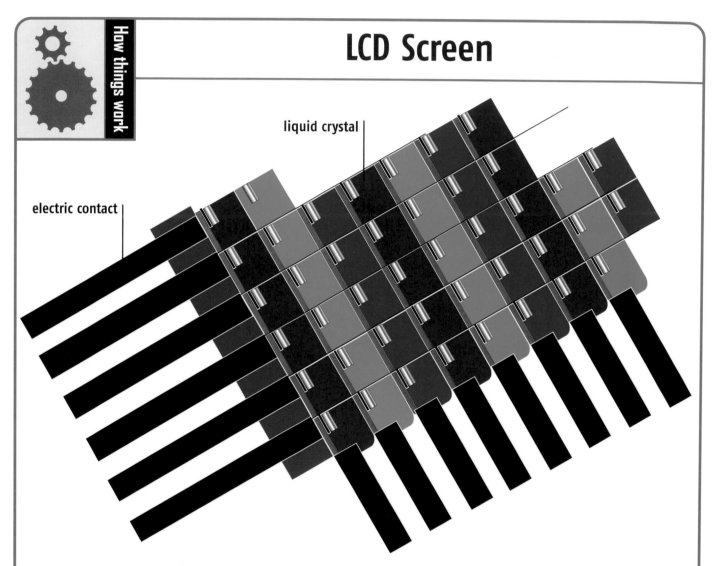

liquid crystal

electric contact

Unlike desktop computers, which generally have large television-style monitors, portable notebook computers have flat, liquid-crystal display (LCD) screens. These build up pictures out of millions of colored segments (above). Each segment is a tiny crystal that can be switched on or off by a tiny electrical current. There are separate crystals for making up the red, green, and blue components of the picture. LCD displays are also used in digital watches, cellphones, and games machines.

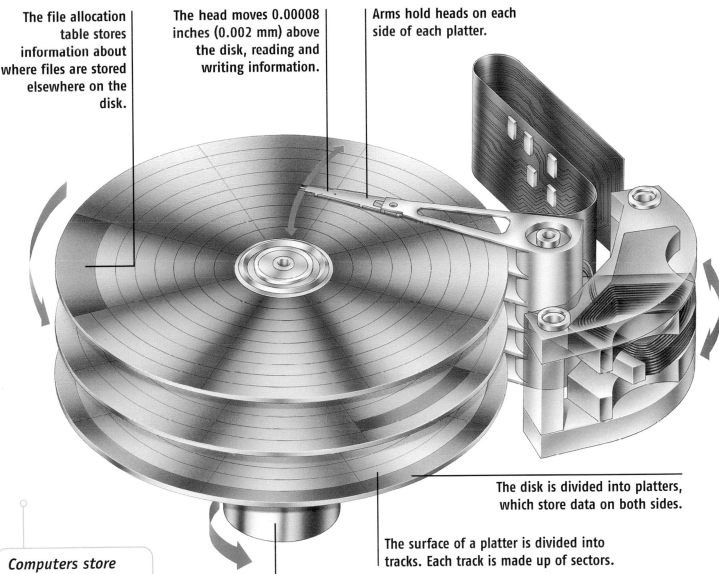

The file allocation table stores information about where files are stored elsewhere on the disk.

The head moves 0.00008 inches (0.002 mm) above the disk, reading and writing information.

Arms hold heads on each side of each platter.

The disk is divided into platters, which store data on both sides.

The surface of a platter is divided into tracks. Each track is made up of sectors.

A motor spins the disk.

Computers store files and programs on a hard disk. This is a piece of rigid magnetic material on which data can be recorded or read back using magnetic heads, similar to those used in a cassette recorder. The disk spins around at high speed so the computer can quickly store and read information from all parts of the disk.

not run programs written for another machine. Even computers from the same manufacturer were sometimes incompatible.

Things improved in 1976 when American teacher and computer scientist Gary Kildall (1942–94) started selling a piece of software called CP/M (Control Program/Microcomputer). It was the first standard operating system for a microcomputer. The program ran from a floppy disk drive and worked on a range of different computers.

The advantage of CP/M was that machines run by it could all load the same off-the-shelf application programs. By 1981, about 200,000 copies of CP/M had been sold to people running 3,000 different types of microcomputer.

At first, companies such as IBM did not take microcomputers very seriously, but the success of the Apple II proved that there was a huge market for small computers. Meanwhile, CP/M was starting to standardize the way microcomputers worked. In 1980, IBM finally realized these new developments were going to threaten its highly profitable mainframe business. IBM decided to act quickly. Within one year, it had developed a rival machine to the Apple II, named the IBM Personal Computer (PC). IBM tried to persuade Gary Kildall to write an operating system, based on CP/M, for the new machine. When he refused, it turned instead to a young Harvard dropout named Bill Gates (born 1955). The program Gates wrote, PC-DOS (Disk Operating System), helped turn the PC into a huge success that soon captured 40 percent of the market.

THE RISE OF WINDOWS

While IBM had been developing its PC for small business customers, Apple had been working on a machine that truly appealed to the masses. Nicknamed the PITS (Person-In-The-Street) computer, this was partly inspired by a revolutionary machine called the Xerox Alto. The Alto was the first personal computer to have a picture-based screen or graphical user interface (GUI). Apple's PITS project eventually led to the launch of its popular Macintosh computer in 1984. Not to be outdone, a few years later Gates and his company, Microsoft, used similar ideas to turn their PC-DOS operating system into an easier-to-use product called Windows. Apple Computers tried

and failed to sue Microsoft for allegedly copying its ideas in a costly four-year court battle.

Meanwhile, other manufacturers, such as Dell and Compaq, had found ways of making machines, known as clones, that did the same things as an IBM PC but sold for much less. IBM was suddenly just one among many manufacturers of PCs. Apple, too, had apparently come to the end of its winning streak: Although the Macintosh remained popular with home users, it never really caught on as a business machine to be used in offices.

The biggest winners were Microsoft. Like those made by IBM, PC clones were still designed to use Microsoft software. The Windows operating system now runs four out of five of the personal computers on the planet, and Bill Gates has become the world's richest man.

A computer mouse controls a cursor on the screen. This cursor is used to activate features and move items around. A mouse has a heavy ball inside it that rolls around as you push it along. Rollers inside detect how the ball moves and send electrical signals to the computer. Using these signals, the computer determines where to place the cursor on the screen. Buttons on the mouse are used to activate the features on the screen.

ball

button

roller

Light beams detect the motion of the rollers.

Graphical User Interface

menu of commands

window

desktop

icons

Early computers were operated in cumbersome ways by turning wheels, connecting plugs, or by feeding in punched cards. By the 1970s, microcomputers could be programmed by typing in simple commands on an ordinary typewriter-like keyboard. But in the 1980s, computers became even easier to use thanks to the graphical user interface (GUI). This is a way of operating computers using pictures instead of words. The GUI was developed in the early 1970s at the Xerox Palo Alto Research Center (PARC). It was first used in a ground-breaking computer called the Xerox Alto, which inspired the design of both the Apple Macintosh and Microsoft Windows. The heart of a GUI (above) is an image of a desktop that fills the computer screen. On the desktop are little pictures (icons) of things like documents, printers, and disks. Instead of typing in complicated commands using the keyboard, the user simply moves icons around the desktop using a mouse.

SOFTWARE

1
2
3
4
5 6 7

Three things are needed to make a computer work properly: Hardware, which includes everything from the computer chips to the monitor, the printer, and all the cables that connect them together; electricity, which provides the energy to make all these things work; and software, or the programs that tell the hardware what to do.

Computer Desktop

The screen of a modern computer is called a desktop. Users can scroll through windows and boxes like they would with paper on a real desk.

1. Computers can be set up for many different users. Once someone logs in, the screen displays what they need.

2. Clicking on these icons will open the internet browser and email.

3. A list of favorite applications.

4. Users can manage the things stored on the hard disk here.

5. Users decorate their desktop with their favorite pictures.

6. Like a real desk, a computer desktop has a recycle bin, where unwanted documents can be thrown away, or deleted.

7. A clock displays the time.

Software is what makes computers different from other machines: Simply by swapping one program for another, a computer can be transformed instantly from a word processor or statistics calculator to a computer games machine or drawing board. It is this tremendous flexibility that makes the computer the most useful tool ever invented.

SYSTEMS AND APPLICATIONS

Computers run two different kinds of software: systems and applications. Systems software controls a computer's most basic operations, such as how words are displayed on the screen, how information is read from a compact disc, and how it communicates with other computers.

The software that controls these things is called the operating system. Most of the world's personal computers run the Microsoft Windows operating system.

Another type of software controls programs such as word processors, graphics packages, web browsers, and so on. These programs are known as applications. The first PCs could run only one application at a time. Modern PCs can run several applications at once by dividing their time between each one, or multitasking.

Binary Numbers

Software is written in a digital code of binary numbers. Instead of counting using ten, or decimal, units (0-9), a computer only understands numbers written in two, or binary, units (0-1)

Name	Decimal units		Binary units			
	10s	1s	8s	4s	2s	1s
ZERO	0	0	0	0	0	0
ONE	0	1	0	0	0	1
TWO	0	2	0	0	1	0
THREE	0	3	0	0	1	1
FOUR	0	4	0	1	0	0
FIVE	0	5	0	1	0	1
SIX	0	6	0	1	1	0
SEVEN	0	7	0	1	1	1
EIGHT	0	8	1	0	0	0
NINE	0	9	1	0	0	1
TEN	1	0	1	0	1	0

The software made by Bill Gates's company Microsoft is used on most computers.

DATA

Computers are often described as information processors. They take in information, transform or process it in different ways, and then print or display the results. For example, you might open a photograph in a graphics program (input), change the brightness or the colors (the processing stage), and then print out the picture (output).

Computers and people speak very different languages, so there has to be some way of turning everyday information into the "computerspeak" of binary 1s and 0s. The solution to this problem is called the American Standard Code for Information Interchange (ASCII), which works like a computer alphabet. ASCII uses the numbers 0–255, which computers can understand, to represent all the different letters, numbers, and symbols that people use.

81

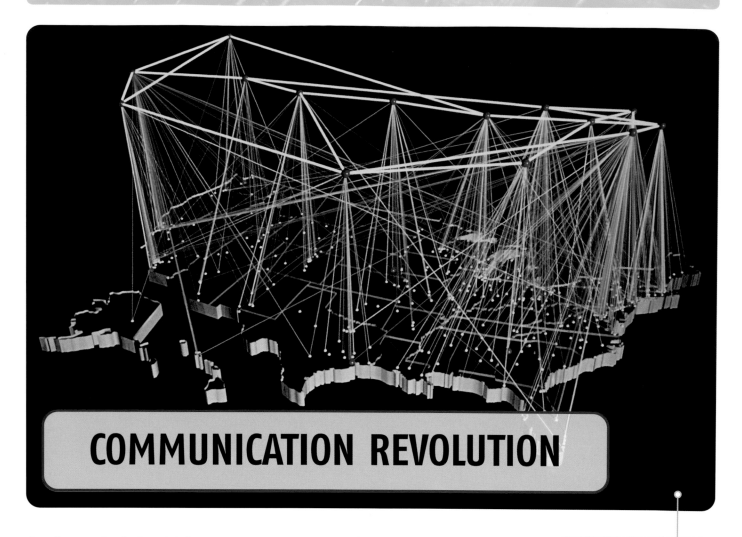

COMMUNICATION REVOLUTION

At the end of the 20th century, computers, television, radio, telephones, and the Internet have all started to be used together. Because of this it is now easier than ever to share information with people anywhere on Earth.

MAKING CONNECTIONS

Computers are extremely useful machines, but they become even more powerful tools when they are connected to form networks. People using networks can work together and share ideas. A group of computers linked together over a small area, such as a workplace or school, is known as a local area network (LAN). Larger networks, or WANs (wide area networks) join LANs together. The biggest computer network of all is the Internet, which currently links together tens of millions of computers all over the planet.

The Internet was born in 1969 out of a U.S. Department of Defense project called Advanced Research Projects Agency Network (ARPAnet). The basic idea was to connect up the many important military computer resources spread around the country, so they did not have to be gathered in one place. In the event of a war or natural disaster, only part of the network would be affected, and other parts could take over.

This map shows the traffic of data flowing through the National Science Foundation Network (NSFNET) in the United States in 1991. This network was one of the first parts of the Internet. The white lines represent the main connections, or backbones. Darker lines show the less busy parts of the network.

Tim Berners-Lee invented the World Wide Web while working at the European particle physics research center CERN.

In 1984, the National Science Foundation set up a network called NSFNET to link American universities together. Other networks joined in, and soon the Internet was born.

INFORMATION SUPPLY

Initially the Internet was used just for sending files and emails back and forth. But people had long believed computers could be used to share other kinds of information. In 1945, computer pioneer Vannevar Bush (1890–1974) had proposed building a machine called the Memex, which could store knowledge in a very structured way by making links between related ideas.

Perhaps Memex was one of the inspirations behind the World Wide Web (WWW), invented in 1989 by British computer scientist Tim Berners-Lee (born 1955).

The Web is a vast collection of documents, called web sites, which are stored on computers connected to the Internet. People can look at these documents through an application called a web browser. Web sites can contain pictures, text, sound, and video.

The Web has grown so fast because of two features: Firstly, web sites can be seen using any computer with a browser. Secondly, like Memex, the features in web pages are connected to each other by clickable links. These

How things work

Email

Email (electronic mail) is a way of sending a typewritten message to another person through a network, or over the Internet. Emails are generally simple text messages coded in ASCII, but they can also include attachments, such as photos, music clips, or documents. They can be sent from anywhere, and emails can be viewed on any size of computer (right) and some cell phones.

An email finds its way to its recipient by using the email address. The address has two parts. The part after the @ ("at" sign) is the domain (the location of the computer network on the Internet). The part before the @ sign is the computer, or email account, on that network to which the email should be delivered.

How things work

Optical Fiber

Optical fibers are plastic-coated strands of glass that transmit huge amounts of information as tiny pulses of light. The light pulses reflect off the boundary between the glass and the plastic cladding. These cables can carry phone calls and data at least 50 times faster than ordinary wire cables. Fiber optics was invented in 1954 by Indian physicist Narinder Kapany.

Single-mode fiber

This type of fiber carries a single signal.

core

Cladding stops light escaping.

protective sheath

steel core

optical fiber

Long-distance cables carry signals with a more controlled reflection.

Multimode fibers

plastic sheath

protective layer

Several signals are reflected off the cladding. This sort of fiber is used in short lengths because the signals do not necessarily arrive at the same time. This is due to the material in the core.

Multimode fibers have a wider core than single-mode fibers.

Fact The light used in optical fibers comes from a light-emitting diode (LED). LEDs produce coherent light, that is, light that forms very clear reflections .

hyperlinks are the threads that knit the global web of information together.

DATA STREAM

Alexander Graham Bell's primitive telephone lines could not have carried songs or videos in the way the Internet does today. Although many Web users still access the Internet using their telephone line, recent developments in communication technology have made it possible for these twisted copper wires to carry a lot more information. For example, a DSL (digital subscriber line) modem can send and receive data at high speeds along copper lines, even when someone is talking on the phone. They do this by sending digital signals at a much higher frequency than the sound of a person's voice.

Fiber-optic cables transmit information as beams of light instead of pulses of electric current. Using fiber optics instead of metal wires greatly increases the bandwidth (the amount of information it can carry) of a cable. The main connections, or backbones, of the Internet, use optical fiber cables that carry 40 million telephone calls at once.

COMING TOGETHER

The communication revolution is blurring the boundaries between different technologies that used to be quite separate. The Internet, for example, is a cross between computer and telephone. People can use their web browsers to watch live television pictures or listen to radio programs that are broadcast through the Internet. Digital memory systems is the innovation that has brought communication technologies together. Once, movies were recorded on celluloid films, music was played from vinyl disks, news was printed on paper, and live television was transmitted by radio waves. Now all these things can be stored, processed, and transmitted by computer.

INTO THE FUTURE

Computers will not necessarily grow any smaller in future, but computing power will shift

This refrigerator has a built-in computer that keeps track of its contents. When it runs out of food, it can automatically order more supplies over the Internet!

increasingly away from traditional desktop machines toward handheld devices and household gadgets. Many cell phones now contain computer-based organizers, or personal digital assistants (PDAs), and digital cameras. Today's portable notebook computers are vastly more powerful than yesterday's desktop PCs. Domestic appliances are also becoming smarter. The Panasonic company recently launched a prototype microwave oven that could suggest things to cook from the contents of the refrigerator. Smart homes, in which even the dogs are robots and the lights come on to the sound of your voice, are becoming increasingly possible. The world's most famous smart home is probably Xanadu, the gadget-packed house built for Bill Gates in Seattle, Washington.

CHANGING WORLD

The communications revolution is changing society in some very interesting ways. Many people now use the Internet to work from home in what is known as telecommuting. Hospitals are

Personal Digital Assistant

Key inventions

PDAs (personal digital assistants) are small handheld, battery-powered computers. Some are little more than address books and diaries. Others are fully fledged, miniature PCs with built-in cell phones. They can hook up to the Internet to send and receive emails or browse the Web. Usually PDAs run a slimmed-down version of the operating system used on PCs and have built-in software such as word processors, spreadsheets, and so on. While some PDAs have a miniature keyboard or keypad, most can recognize handwriting if it is traced onto their screen with a pen (left).

Key inventions

MP3

MP3 is a way of storing high-quality music on computers. The sound information is compressed so, although an MP3 file sounds just as good as music from a CD, it takes up a tenth of the space. These small files are sent easily through the Internet. Many people share music files with each other (above). Soon people will buy their music as MP3 files. The cost might depend on how popular a song is and how long the purchaser wishes to keep it.

testing remote-controlled robots that can operate on patients under the control of a surgeon in another state, country, or continent through high-bandwidth optical-fiber links. The use of paper money is starting to disappear in some places as credit cards with built-in microchips take over. In Hong Kong, 9 million people already use smart cards to pay for trips on public transportation.

Sharing information will become even easier in the future as the world becomes ever more heavily connected and technologies continue to converge. Today's libraries are already being replaced by digital libraries that you can access over the Internet. In the future, people are likely to download movies, books, and music whenever they need them. They no longer need to borrow them from video stores or libraries or keep their own collections.

Technologies such as satellites, cell phones and the Internet have already made the world seem a much smaller place. It is as easy to buy goods from a web site on the other side of the world as from the store down the street.

Some people think this could reduce the diversity of the world and make it a more boring place. Others argue that, far from narrowing things down, the Internet gives us access to far more things than ever before.

Technology is always a force for change, sometimes good and sometimes bad. No one can ever predict what impact inventions will have on society. But as communications technology continues to spread around the globe, it does at least have the power to bring people together, help them understand one another, and make the world a prosperous and peaceful place.

WIRELESS INTERNET

Up till now, Internet access has only really been possible where there are telephones and, in many places, old-fashioned cables and exchanges restrict the speed at which information can flow back and forth. A fast-growing new type of Internet access, wireless Internet, promises to solve both these problems by freeing the Internet from the telephone.

WAP PHONES

Cell phones offer the simplest way to give people access to the Internet while they are away from their home or office. WAP (Web Access Protocol) cell phones contain mini-web browsers, which can be used to look at slimmed-down web pages. Although they were launched with great excitement, they have failed to capture people's imagination because they are slow to use. A cell phone screen can show only a tiny amount of information, and even PDAs with built-in cell phones can only display small parts of ordinary web pages.

One alternative is to use a cell phone to connect an ordinary notebook computer

So-called third-generation cell phones can send and receive video. As well as seeing the people you call, you can also watch sports highlights and short clips.

to the Internet but, even then, data passes back and forth at less than a fifth of the speed of an ordinary land-line telephone connection.

WiFi HOTSPOTS

Wireless Fidelity (WiFi) offers a much better alternative to the problem. All around the world, public places such as cafés, libraries, shopping malls, and railroad stations are being set up as so-called WiFi "hotspots" that provide very fast wireless access to the Internet. People who want to use the Internet at a hotspot have to have a special WiFi card fitted into their laptop. This sends data back and forth to a base station at the hotspot using radio waves. Unlike a laptop connected to the Internet by a cell phone, WiFi is an example of broadband Internet. It works at about 40 times the speed of an ordinary land-line connection.

WiFi "hotspots" are useful for traveling business people. They do not have to visit offices to do their job. They can meet customers in public places, such as a cafe or an airport to discuss business. In the hotspot, they can connect to their company network with the high-speed Internet service.

WIRELESS BROADBAND

Many people would like to upgrade their Internet connection to broadband, but they live in a remote part of the world, too far away from cable services. High-speed telephone services such as DSL become slower over long distances, and users need to live about 3 miles (5 km) from the telephone exchange. The net result is that while some parts of the world are racing ahead on the "information superhighway," others remain stuck in a rut. Wireless broadband working in a similar way to cellular phone network offers a way out of this problem by making it possible to get high-speed access to rural areas.

Time Line

3300 B.C.E.
Sumerians develop the first written language.

1700 B.C.E.
Semitic peoples develop the first alphabet.

1812
Charles Babbage begins to design programmable computers.

1837
The first electric telegraphs are developed.

1851
Morse code becomes a worldwide standard for communications.

1876
The telephone is invented by Alexander Graham Bell.

▲ 3300 B.C.E.

▲ 1800 C.E.

1450
Gutenberg develops the first printing press using movable metal type.

105 C.E.
Chinese people invent paper.

59 B.C.E.
Julius Caesar publishes the first newspaper.

1839
Louis Daguerre and William Henry Fox Talbot invent photography.

1888
George Eastman launches the Kodak camera.

1877
Thomas Alva Edison invents a sound-recording machine.

1895
The Lumière brothers invent the movie projector and open the first movie theater.

1901
Guglielmo Marconi makes the first transatlantic radio transmission.

1969
U.S. Department of Defense designs ARPANET computer network.

1976
Steve Jobs and Steve Wozniak develop the first Apple computer. Gary Kildall invents the first computer disk operating system, CP/M.

2003
Handheld devices that can send and receive video images, make phone calls, handle emails, and access the Web become widely available.

▲
1900

▲
2000

1954
Fiber optics is invented by Narinder Kapany.

1947
The transistor is invented.

1923
John Logie Baird transmits the first television picture.

1989
Tim Berners-Lee invents the World Wide Web.

1981
IBM releases the Personal Computer.

Glossary

amplifier An electronic component that increases the strength of an electrical signal.

analog A way of representing information using cogs, wheels or other physical measurements.

antenna A metal mast that can send and receive radio waves.

broadband A type of high-capacity communication link.

cathode-ray tube The main component of a television set that makes the picture.

data The information processed by a computer.

digital A way of representing information with numbers.

fiber optic A thin glass tube that transmits information in the form of light pulses.

hardware The physical equipment that makes up a computer system.

mainframe A very large and usually very powerful computer.

modulation A way of coding a television or radio signal in an electromagnetic wave.

movable type A set of metal letters that can be rearranged to print different pages.

photocell An electronic component that detects light. Also called a photoelectric cell.

pictography Representing words using pictures.

punched card A piece of cardboard containing information in a pattern of punched holes.

receiver An electronic item that receives and decodes television or radio signals.

satellite A spacecraft that transmits communications signals from one side of Earth to the other.

semaphore A way of sending information between two places, usually with flags or hand signals.

software The instructions that operate a computer.

telegraph A way of sending messages down a cable.

transistor An electronic switch used in computer circuits.

vacuum tube A type of electronic switch.

wireless Communication with radio waves instead of cables.

Further Resources

Books

Fire in the Valley: The Making of the Personal Computer by Paul Freiberger and Michael Swaine. McGraw-Hill Trade, 1999.

Inventing the Internet by Janet Abbate. MIT Press, 2000.

Connecting Civilization: The Growth of Communication by Dennis Karwatka. Prakken Publications, 2003.

Web Sites

Smithsonian: Computers and Communications

http://www.si.edu/science_and_technology/computers_and_communications/

Index

Page numbers in **bold** refer to feature spreads; those in *italics* refer to picture captions.

Picture Credits